THE VAN GOGH MUSEUM   *Paintings and Pastels*

Paintings and Pastels

THE VAN GOGH MUSEUM

Ronald de Leeuw

Waanders Publishers | Zwolle

Contents

Introduction

The Van Gogh Museum

When, during a three-day excursion to Amsterdam in October 1885, Vincent van Gogh paid a visit to the recently opened Rijksmuseum, the young artist could not possibly have imagined that in less than a century, on 2 June 1973, an entire museum on Amsterdam's Museumplein would be dedicated to his own artistic legacy. In the two decades that have elapsed since its foundation, the Van Gogh Museum has grown into one of the most popular institutions of its kind in Europe, a place of pilgrimage for millions seeking the unique experience of standing face to face with one of the nineteenth century's most fascinating artists.

Though it was in France that Van Gogh lived and worked from 1886, and there that he carved out a place for himself in the annals of Post-impressionism, only a modest portion of his prodigious oeuvre remained in that country. After the artist's death, his brother Theo's widow took most of the unsold drawings and pictures back with her to Holland. Thanks in part to the superb collection that Hélène Kröller-Müller amassed in the early twentieth century, over a third of the master's oeuvre found a permanent home in his native land. Besides the museum that bears his name, the municipal museums of Amsterdam, The Hague and Rotterdam, as well as numerous smaller museums scattered about Holland, proudly preserve important Van Goghs.

The collection of the Van Gogh Museum in Amsterdam is far and away the largest and most representative of the artist's oeuvre. It includes seven sketchbooks and some six hundred original letters from Vincent to Theo, in addition to over two hundred paintings and 580 drawings, all on permanent loan from the Vincent van Gogh Foundation. The Museum also houses work by friends and colleagues which Theo, who dealt in art, and Vincent either purchased or acquired through exchange. This so-called Theo van Gogh Collection makes it possible to present the oeuvre of Vincent van Gogh in a broader context, while forming in turn the basis of the Museum's acquisition policy. Over the past few years the Van Gogh Museum has been actively redefining itself as an institution where, with Van Gogh as the pivotal figure, a broad swath of European art of the later nineteenth century is presented in all its diversity. In this respect the Museum forms an ideal link between its neighbours on the Museumplein: the Rijksmuseum, devoted primarily to Dutch fine and applied art up to approximately 1900, and the Stedelijk Museum, with its international twentieth-century collection.

At the time the Van Gogh Museum was founded, a museum dedicated to a single artist was still something of an anomaly. Since then the foundation of the Musée Picasso in Paris has

Meijer de Haan,
Portrait drawing of
Theo van Gogh
(1857-1891) in 1889

Official opening of the Van Gogh Museum by H.M. Queen Juliana on 2 June 1973

dispelled any lingering doubts about the formula of the 'one-man museum' – provided, of course, that the appeal of the artist is sufficiently universal and that the quality of the collection does justice to his art. Indeed it is a rare, if not unique, luxury to be able to plumb the creative process of a great master so deeply in a single location – though one could hardly say the rest of the world is bereft of Van Gogh's work! Of the more than nine hundred pictures the artist is estimated to have painted in the course of his brief career, two thirds have found their way into public and private collections from Moscow to Melbourne, and from Toronto to Sao Paulo.

Amsterdam, however, is home to the core of Vincent's oeuvre. In the Van Gogh Museum there are entire ensembles from every period of the artist's creativity. The Brabant period is particularly well represented: almost all the major works, including the definitive version of *The Potato Eaters*, are still together, as is nearly everything Van Gogh is known to have painted during his brief Antwerp sojourn in 1885-86. Thanks to no less than eighty-five canvases, including an impressive series of eighteen self-portraits, the stylistic metamorphosis Van Gogh underwent in Paris can be studied here better than anywhere else. From Vincent's Arles period the Museum possesses such major works as *The Bedroom*, *The Yellow House*, the *Sunflowers* and what may well be his loveliest landscape, *Harvest at La Crau*. While this group is notably rich in landscapes, figure pieces and portraits are few and far between. There is unfortunately no *Arlésienne*, no *Berceuse*, no *Postman Roulin*. The artist's convalescence in St-Rémy is worthily represented by *The Reaper*, the *Vase with Irises* and the *Branches of an Almond Tree in Blossom*. Nor can so many of his unique copies after his favourite painter Millet be found

anywhere but Amsterdam. Four of the principal canvases from the last month of Van Gogh's life in Auvers form an impressive finale to the display: the atmospheric *View of the Castle of Auvers*, the revolutionary *Tree Roots*, the menacing *Landscape with Stormy Sky* and the *Cornfield with Crows* – formerly taken to be his swan song.

The caretakers of the estate

When Vincent van Gogh died in July 1890 he did not leave a will. In August 1890, however, his sisters Anna, Elisabeth and Willemien agreed that his brother Theo would inherit the entire estate. After all, Theo had supported Vincent for many years, thus enabling him to pursue an artistic career. When Theo died in turn on 25 January 1891, on behalf of his widow the sisters formally renounced any claim to the brothers' collection. Shortly thereafter Jo van Gogh-Bonger decided to leave Paris, and to take her infant son Vincent Willem to her native Holland. She settled in Bussum, where she took in lodgers and translated for a living. As the widow of an art dealer, she naturally supplemented her income by selling works from the collection from time to time. In 1901 Jo married the painter and critic Johan Cohen Gosschalk, who wholeheartedly supported her tireless struggle to promote her late brother-in-law's art. In 1903 the family moved to

Johan Cohen Gosschalk, Jo van Gogh-Bonger (1862-1925) at her writing table

Jo Bonger, Johan Cohen Gosschalk and Vincent Willem van Gogh in the sittingroom of their house on Brachthuyzerstraat in Amsterdam, ca. 1905

Isaac Israëls, Vincent Willem van Gogh in Hyde Park, London, August 1914

Amsterdam. Cohen Gosschalk took an active part in organising the large Van Gogh exhibition at the Stedelijk Museum, which helped establish the artist's reputation. In 1910 the family returned to the country, where Cohen Gosschalk died in 1912. In 1914 Jo van Gogh-Bonger, who had reassumed her first husband's name in the meantime, put the finishing touches on what could well be called her life's work, an edition of the entire corpus of Vincent's letters to Theo. After completing his training as a civil engineer, in 1915 Jo and Theo's son, Vincent Willem, married Josina Wibaut. He was determined to demonstrate his own professional merits before becoming more actively involved with the Van Gogh Collection – which he had already begun to do while his mother was still alive. With few exceptions, nothing more was sold after Jo van Gogh died in 1925. In 1927 Dr Vincent Willem van Gogh and his wife settled in Laren, after their residence 't Lanthuys (The Country House), into which Jo had moved in 1910, had been radically remodelled. Twenty of Van Gogh's most famous pictures, most of them mounted in flat white frames, served as decoration; the rest were kept in a makeshift storage room. This situation changed in 1930, following another major exhibition at the Stedelijk Museum of works from the collections of Dr van Gogh and Hélène Kröller-Müller. When the exhibition closed, the former was asked to allow his Van Goghs to be displayed in the Stedelijk on a permanent basis. On 5 November 1930, thanks in part to the insistence of Josina van Gogh-Wibaut, the Van Gogh family and the Municipality reached a formal agreement to this effect. With the exception of the war years – when the collection was hidden in the dunes near the small town of Castricum – much of the collection was hung there on a semi-permanent basis. Dr van Gogh presented his uncle's *Berceuse* to the Stedelijk in gratitude for the Museum's care of the collection during the war.

In close consultation with the successive directors of the Stedelijk Museum, after World War II Vincent Willem began organising exhibitions of the collection in Europe, the United States and Canada during the winter months, which considerably enhanced Vincent's international renown. Eventually Dr van Gogh realised that if appropriate steps were not taken, the collection would be irretrievably dispersed after his death. In late 1959 H.J. Reinink, Director-General for the Arts at the Ministry of Education, Arts and Sciences, presented the engineer with a detailed proposal. The plan envisaged a museum especially for the collection in Amsterdam, which would be provided by the Dutch state. To this end the Vincent van Gogh Foundation was founded on 10

Vincent van Gogh, La Berceuse, Stedelijk Museum, Amsterdam

July 1960. Besides Dr Vincent Willem van Gogh, his second wife and his three children, a state representative also sits on the board. With the consent of the Dutch parliament, the state purchased the entire collection on behalf of the Foundation in 1962. The Municipality of Amsterdam furnished the land for the museum on Museumplein.

Sketch designs for the Van Gogh Museum by Gerrit Rietveld, June 1963

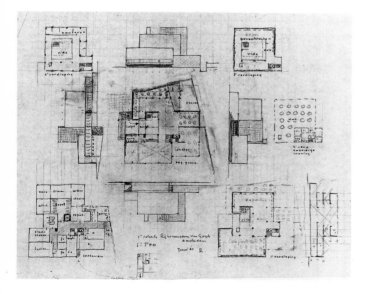

The Museum

In 1963 Dr van Gogh met for the first time with the architect of his choice, Gerrit Rietveld, one of the foremost exponents of the De Stijl movement, which had flourished in the 1920s. Frank Lloyd Wright's recently completed Guggenheim Museum in New York formed an important source of inspiration, as did the Maison de la Culture in Le Havre by Le Corbusier's pupil Audigier, noted for its flexible arrangement of space and natural lighting. In 1964 Rietveld died, however, as did his successor, J. van Dillen, in 1966. At that point their associate J. van Tricht was contracted for the definitive design of the building and its interior. The original plan was to cover the Museum with off-white glazed (or clinker) bricks and brownish grey enamelled steel sheets. For various, primarily practical reasons this plan was abandoned, however, in favour of grey blocks composed of concrete chips; this accounts for the massive, impregnable appearance of the building from the street.

Given the somewhat forbidding exterior, visitors are all the more surprised by the interior of the Museum, with its series of airy, interconnected spaces flooded with daylight from an immense central well covered with glass. The well creates an extraordinary spatial effect that is conducive to an uninhibited, relaxed encounter with the works of art. This same central column of air enables the building, originally designed for sixty to eighty thousand visitors per year, to accommodate over ten times that number with none of the claustrophobia one would expect.

The founders' original intention had been to display the relatively dark works from Vincent's Brabant period on the ground floor, and the sunnier canvases from the French period on the higher floors, nearer the skylight, but for various reasons this proved impractical. As things now stand a rotating selection of nineteenth-century pictures is usually displayed on the ground floor of the Museum, while the monumental first floor is entirely given over to a chronological presentation of the artist's principal works. This enables the visitor to follow Van Gogh's development through the various stages of his life, as he moved from Nuenen to Antwerp, then on to Paris, Arles, St-Rémy and finally to Auvers-sur-Oise.

Originally the second floor, which is protected from daylight, was set aside for a permanent selection of Vincent's drawings and for the collection of Japanese prints he and Theo

Exterior of the Van Gogh Museum seen from Museumplein

assembled. But since the increasingly stringent international standards of collection management militate against exposing works on paper to light, however weak, for extended periods of time, Van Gogh's drawings are now displayed only in temporary exhibitions. Even stricter rules apply to his extremely fragile letters. Written for the most part in corrosive iron gall ink on inexpensive paper, these brittle sheets are exceedingly fragile. Only for the centenary of the artist's death in 1990 was an exception made, when all the illustrated letters were featured in a moving exhibition. Part of the space on the second floor is now reserved for a study collection: a wide selection of Van Gogh's minor works which are usually kept in storage, presented informally. In 1990, during the large-scale retrospective exhibition commemorating the 100th anniversary of Vincent's death, no less than 865,000 visitors visited the Museum. Not only the air conditioning but also the lighting of the building had to be specially adapted for the occasion. As we noted in the case of graphic art, the amount of light to which oil paintings may be exposed has also been greatly reduced since the building's construction in 1973. Under the guidance of the architect Frank Wintermans, a number of aesthetic adjustments were made to the interior on that occasion. A layer of stucco was applied to the walls of the central, glass-covered well to give it a more streamlined appearance, for instance.

The two most dominant structural elements of the building – the stairways in the glass-covered centre of the building and on the side facing Museumplein – serve to channel the flow of visitors. That in the centre enables one to experience the interior as a whole, while that on the side commands a fine view of Museumplein. Each floor can also be reached by lift, so that the building is fully accessible to the handicapped. As it was designed by Rietveld, Van Dillen and Van Tricht, the Museum has coped remarkably well under the circumstances. Every building has its limits, however. The steadily rising tide of visitors has left no choice but to add a wing. Their numbers

Letter from Vincent van Gogh to Theo, Arles, May 1888

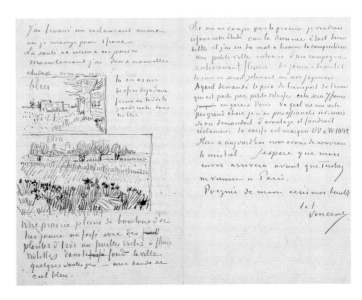

INTRODUCTION

The study collection on the second floor of the Van Gogh Museum

have grown by an average of fifty thousand every year since 1985, mostly concentrated during the summer months. In order to guarantee every interested individual an equally rewarding, relaxed visit, more square feet are required. From the mid-1980s the rapid succession of temporary exhibitions exacerbated the need for space designated especially for this purpose.

In late 1989 the Amsterdam City Council granted the Van Gogh Museum permission to expand on the side facing Museumplein. In the autumn of 1991, the financial basis for the expansion was laid when 37.5 million Dutch guilders were donated by the Yasuda Fire & Marine Insurance Company Ltd., the same Japanese insurance firm that had caused an international sensation several years earlier when it purchased one of the three versions of Van Gogh's *Still Life with Sunflowers* for a record sum. The company's donation to the Museum underscores its association with the artist, who is immensely popular in Japan. The Japanese architect Kisho Kurokawa was asked to design the new exhibition wing.

The evolution of the collection since 1973

Acquisitions are the lifeblood of every museum. A collection is a living organism fed constantly by new impulses, a repository of art and knowledge that constantly grows and improves. Be it a museum with a historically defined parameter such as our own or a museum of contemporary art, this process continues indefinitely. Since most Dutch museums have done very little collecting in the field of international nineteenth-century painting in recent decades, the Van Gogh Museum decided to accept the challenge.

In formulating an acquisition policy, the Museum has taken the character of the core collection as its point of departure, acquiring works consistent with or complementary to the collection the Van Gogh brothers assembled. The brothers' correspondence tells us a great deal about their taste, thus forming an invaluable guideline. In a more general sense, the Museum also seeks to enrich the artistic patrimony of the Netherlands in the field of European painting from the period 1840-1920. The related collection of the H.W. Mesdag Museum in The Hague, administered by the Van Gogh Museum since 1990, influences the acquisition policy as well. Vincent and Theo van Gogh lacked both the time and the means that would have enabled their instincts as collectors to mature. In the span of a few short years they amassed what

Kisho Kurokawa, Design for the expansion of the Van Gogh Museum (1991)

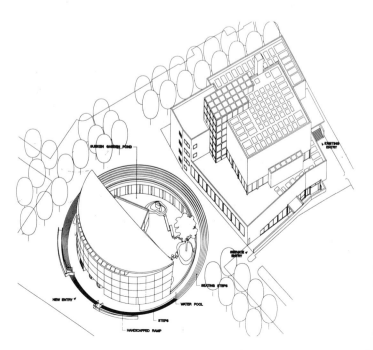

could be described as a typical artist's collection, consisting largely of works acquired through exchange with colleagues both known (Bernard, Gauguin, Guillaumin, Pissarro and Toulouse-Lautrec) and less known (Boggs, Jeannin, Laval, Russell and Vignon). Only a small portion of their collection – the groups of works by Monticelli and Gauguin, the Manet prints and the splendid Seurat drawing – was actually purchased. We know the brothers regretted not having managed to exchange work with a number of the most prominent Impressionists, and that Vincent was keen to have an oil sketch by Seurat. Yet their promising start was abruptly halted by their respective deaths in July 1890 and January 1891. Though the collection was subsequently cherished by Theo's widow and son, who lent generously to exhibitions, and though from 1930 the Stedelijk Museum displayed many of Vincent's works, the collection as a whole was inaccessible and its growth was stunted.

With the opening of the Van Gogh Museum in 1973, it finally became possible to study and enjoy the collection in its entirety, with all its strengths and weaknesses. Thanks to Dr van Gogh's foresight, this was one private collection that made the transition to a museum without being allowed to fossilise. From the outset he took the position that the collection was a living organism that needed to grow. Between 1962 and his death in 1978 he was actively involved in purchasing works by Van Gogh and his contemporaries, to the extent that he occasionally advanced his own funds when government approval took too long. Besides the half dozen drawings and several small paintings by Van Gogh that he acquired for the Museum, he successfully sollicited a number of gifts and legacies. As a result, the Van Gogh Museum could present its namesake as an artist engaged in a lively dialogue with the art of his age, as opposed to 'le grand isolé'.

In the years that immediately followed the Museum's opening, Van Gogh's work did not fetch the sort of astronomical sums regularly reported in the press nowadays, and an occasional acquisition was still within the realm of possibility. In 1977 the Museum purchased Vincent's *Poplars in the Autumn* from his Nuenen period and in 1979 the powerful portrait drawing *The Zouave*. Since such acquisitions were long since out of the question by 1990, that year's bequest of two small pictures from the estate of Mrs E. Ribbius Peletier, which Dr van Gogh had arranged before he died, was particularly gratifying. Most works that enter the Museum nowadays are acquired with funds generated by the museum shop. In addition

Georges Seurat, A l'Eden-Concert - 1887

purchases are made with the support of the Vincent van Gogh Foundation. On several occasions an appeal has been made to the Vereniging Rembrandt or to the Ministry of Welfare, Public Health and Culture. The Museum has also received gifts and bequests from private individuals, the business community and the Friends of the Van Gogh Museum Foundation.

The acquisition policy of the Van Gogh Museum places the greatest emphasis on foreign, especially French art of the period 1840-1920. As for Dutch art, only the principal masters of the Hague School and several of Van Gogh's contemporaries are displayed in dialogue, as it were, with their foreign confrères. The Museum has acquired Jozef Israëls's *Peasant Family at Table* (which inspired *The Potato Eaters*), Van Rappard's *Old Woman from Drenthe*, Matthijs Maris's poetic masterpiece *The Girl with the Goats* and Jan Toorop's youthful *Self Portrait*, for instance.
A concentrated collection such as that of the Van Gogh Museum stands to benefit from reinforcing the various nuclei and from expanding the range. Besides the works of Van Gogh himself, the group by such Post-impressionists as

Vincent van Gogh, The Zouave
Arles, June 1888 - F 1443

Gauguin, Bernard, Toulouse-Lautrec and Laval – whom Vincent dubbed 'les impressionnistes du petit boulevard' – forms the essential core of the collection. Thanks to the gift of Elin Ekström in 1990, Emile Bernard is now much better represented. Originally Vincent's painter friends Louis Anquetin and Paul Signac were not represented in the collection. With the recent acquisition of Anquetin's canvas *Le Paysan* and the pastels *Un Bateau* and *Portrait of Emile Bernard*, as well as the purchase of a pre-Pointillist town view by Paul Signac, this gap was filled.

Two acquisition areas that have received particular attention are Realism and Symbolism. While the Museum still has to do without a picture by Millet, it boasts important pieces by his colleagues Jules Breton, Jozef Israëls and Léon Lhermitte, who likewise specialised in the peasant genre. The Museum was also able to procure both a handsome pastel self-portrait and a representative oil painting by Millet's urban counterpart Jean-François Raffaëlli, the painter of Parisian suburban life who exhibited for years along with the Impressionists. Fine pieces have also been acquired by Philippe Rousseau and François Bonvin, minor masters of the realistic still life, whose art ironically enough is satirised by another recent acquisition, Thomas Couture's *Le Réaliste* of 1865.

Over the past few years the Van Gogh Museum has taken steps to form a small Symbolist ensemble. The stimulus to do so was formed by the acquisition of two splendid pastels by Odilon Redon from the former Andries Bonger Collection, in 1986 and 1987. Since then the presentation of the exquisite – and sometimes also slightly morbid – Symbolist art of the

1890s has been further stimulated by the purchase of works by Edmond Aman-Jean, Eugène Carrière, Maurice Denis, Louis Welden Hawkins, Fernand Khnopff and Carlos Schwabe. The Museum counts itself particularly fortunate to have been able to form an ensemble of three pictures and several drawings by Pierre Puvis de Chavannes in a relatively short period of time. Puvis came to mean a great deal to Van Gogh during the last months of his life. At long last he is worthily represented in Holland by a large painted sketch for one of his principal works, a mural devoted to the life of Sainte Geneviève in the Panthéon. The scant representation of true Impressionist masters remains a thorn in the Museum's side. To be sure, several charming works by Claude Emile Schuffenecker and two harbingers of Impressionism, Paul Guigou and Johan Barthold Jongkind, have helped ease the pain, but the great masters of the movement are simply beyond our financial reach. When, therefore, in 1991 the Rijksdienst Beeldende Kunst lent Claude Monet's *Tulip Field* of 1886, our joy was that much more intense.

This is not to say that marginal masters are not welcome in the Van Gogh Museum. On the contrary, we are only too eager to have them whenever the content and quality of their work enriches our panorama of late nineteenth-century art. This explains, for instance, the purchase of an atmospheric canvas by the Austrian Felician Freiherr von Myrbach, showing the interior of a shop, and that of a suggestive genre portrait of a fashionable young woman by another foreigner working in Paris, the Italian Vittorio Corcos. It was not long before the latter became one of the most popular works in the collection.

Much progress has been made over the past few years toward forming a collection of pastels. This painterly branch of graphic art blossomed in the second half of the nineteenth century, as now evidenced in the Museum by Anquetin, Breitner, Gauguin, Khnopff, Lautrec, Lévy, Pissarro, Point, Redon and Ph. Rousseau. Regrettably, we still lack work in this medium by such luminaries as Cassatt, Degas, Manet and Vuillard.

Loans

In cases where the Van Gogh Museum itself has not managed to redress individual lacunae, we have already cited several examples of permanent loans that served this purpose. The dozens of works with which we were entrusted in 1991 by the Rijksmuseum, the Amsterdams Historisch Museum, the

Rijksmuseum Kröller-Müller and the Rijksdienst Beeldende Kunst have enriched the Museum significantly. Most of the artists, such as Corot, Courbet, Daubigny, Daumier, Decamps, Delacroix, Diaz, Fantin-Latour, Millet and Scheffer, were active around the mid-nineteenth century. Thanks to the generosity of its sister institutions, the Museum can now illustrate the artistic wellsprings on which Van Gogh drew, and the public is able to enjoy works of art that have never been displayed on a permanent basis.

Documentation and scientific research

As well as the numerous sketchbooks, drawings and paintings of Vincent van Gogh, the Van Gogh Museum houses virtually all of the letters the artist ever sent his brother Theo. It preserves his scrapbooks, several of the albums he filled with poetry for his brother, and the hundreds of magazine illustrations he accumulated as a source of inspiration throughout his life. The Vincent van Gogh Foundation has lent the Museum a great deal of correspondence and archival material relating to Theo van Gogh and other members of his family. The archive of the Belgian Van Gogh connoisseur Mark Edo Tralbaut has been moved to the Museum, moreover. Last but not least, there is an extensive library, which is especially strong in late nineteenth-century art; the library was immeasurably enriched in 1992, when the library of the Amsterdam artist's association Arti et Amicitiae was added to it. These various holdings make the Van Gogh Museum the preeminent place to study the artist and the reception of his oeuvre.

Starting in 1970 – that is, three years before the opening of the Museum – results of research carried out by the staff were routinely published in the *Bulletin Vincent*, for which the Van Gogh connoisseur Dr Jan Hulsker was largely responsible. By the time the *Bulletin* was discontinued in 1976, a total of sixteen issues had seen the light. In 1988, in collaboration with the Vincent van Gogh Foundation, the Museum launched a scholarly series entitled *Cahiers Vincent*, featuring previously unpublished sources that contribute in some way to our understanding of the artist. Individual *Cahiers* have included everything from poetry albums assembled by Vincent in the 1870s for his brother and various friends, to letters of condolence Theo received following his brother's death and research into the early provenance of Van Gogh's work. A study of Vincent's painting technique

Emile Bernard, Portrait of Andries Bonger, his wife and Emile Bernard - 1908

and materials has also appeared in the series.

Every year the Van Gogh Museum receives literally hundreds of requests for authentications of works of art from people hoping to hear they own a genuine Van Gogh, the vast majority of which are disappointed. The fact is that most of the submissions are all too patently unworthy of the artist, and indeed some prove to have been intentionally falsified. By the end of the last century Van Gogh's reputation was already such that it was worth forging his work.

Jo van Gogh and her son published what would remain the standard edition of Van Gogh's letters until 1973. That year Dr van Gogh ushered the last reprinting through the press, in time for the opening of the Rijksmuseum Vincent van Gogh. He himself was interested in editing the group of forty-five letters Gauguin wrote Vincent, Theo and Jo van Gogh, now preserved in the Museum, but could not finish the task before he died in 1978. Douglas Cooper finally published the correspondence in 1983, in co-operation with the Museum. In 1990 the staff of the Museum published a completely revised, Dutch-language edition of all known letters to and from Vincent van Gogh, based on new transcriptions. Since then they have been preparing a fully annotated edition of the entire correspondence, and there are also plans for a new catalogue raisonné of Van Gogh's oeuvre.

*Letter of Paul Gauguin to Vincent van Gogh
from ca. 8 November 1889*

Exhibitions

After the opening of the Van Gogh Museum, the first director, Emile Meijer, was quick to introduce the fledgling institution to Amsterdam. Rather than limiting himself to Van Gogh and nineteenth-century art, he launched a wide range of activities, including concerts and theatrical productions. Mikis Theodorakis presented an anthology of his poetry in the Museum, and World Press Photo organised several of its annual exhibitions there as well. In the framework of a visual arts workshop the first courses were offered to the public on drawing, painting and photography.

During Johannes van der Wolk's tenure as director (1978-1982), the Museum charted a more strictly art historical

Sketchbooks of Vincent van Gogh

course. In conformity with the intentions of the founders, two important exhibitions – *Vincent van Gogh in his Dutch Years* (1980) and *Van Gogh and the Birth of Cloisonnism* (1981) – shed valuable light on the artistic context in which Van Gogh worked. The Van Gogh retrospective exhibition in 1990, which was organised in co-operation with the Rijksmuseum Kröller-Müller, was of course a milestone in this respect. The artist was also featured in such exhibitions as *Van Gogh & Millet* (1989) and *Van Gogh and Modern Art 1890-1914* (1990), but by the time Ronald de Leeuw became director in 1986, the Museum's focus had expanded to include the entire second half of the nineteenth century, which it approached, moreover, not from a Dutch or French, but from an international perspective. The Van Gogh Museum also collaborated on numerous exhibitions abroad, including pioneering Van Gogh exhibitions in Toronto, New York, Paris and Arles. The Museum itself organised exhibitions in Italy and Japan, often in co-operation with the Rijksmuseum Kröller-Müller.

Most exhibitions in the Van Gogh Museum naturally revolve around French artists, who set the tone in nineteenth-century Europe, after all, as well as the standard by which Van Gogh judged art: 'don't they form the heart of this century as far as painting is concerned?' he asked. Yet the Museum also devotes attention to art from other European cultural centres from time to time, as in *Ottocento Novecento* and *Glasgow 1900*, which featured late nineteenth-century Italian and Glaswegian art respectively.

The Van Gogh Museum has always taken a particular interest in artists whose work has rarely if ever been shown in the Netherlands, such as Emile Bernard, Adolphe Monticelli, Anton van Rappard, Philippe Rousseau, John Russell, Arnold Schönberg, Walter Sickert, August Strindberg, Felix Vallotton, Jan Verkade, Edouard Vuillard and Stanislaw Witkiewicz. But it has mounted several major exhibitions of well-known masters as well, such as *Monet in Holland* and *French Masters from the Metropolitan Museum*. Whenever possible of course the Museum likes to highlight its own collection, to introduce the public to recent acquisitions, for instance.

Since the mid-1980s, the Museum has also frequently focused on facets of late nineteenth-century graphic art, which went through so many turbulent innovations. It has been privileged to collaborate on such projects with, for instance, the Jane Voorhees Zimmerlee Museum in New Brunswick, the Bibliothèque Nationale in Paris and the Josefowitz Collection. Monographic exhibitions have addressed the graphic oeuvre of such artists as Honoré Daumier, Edvard Munch, Félicien Rops, Henri de Toulouse-Lautrec and James McNeill Whistler, while retrospectives have examined the graphic art of the School of Pont-Aven and the Nabis, besides such publications as *L'Estampe originale* and those of the Nederlandsche Etsclub. Regular visitors to the Van Gogh Museum could thus become well acquainted with late nineteenth-century prints.

Selections from the Museum's own collection of works on paper are also regularly presented, such as Manet prints or English wood engravings originally acquired by the Van Gogh brothers. Japanese graphic art and Japonisme are commonly featured; after all, Van Gogh was one of the principal exponents of the island nation's art, which captivated the contemporary European art world. In 1978 Dr W. van Gulik prepared an initial catalogue of the Museum's own collection of Japanese woodcuts. Then in 1991 a new edition of the catalogue, which was entirely revised and supplemented, was published by Charlotte van Rappard.

When the Van Gogh Museum was established, Dr van Gogh stipulated that it operate according to the most advanced standards, but he was equally concerned that it be a lively institution. Visitors should be confronted not only with the work of Van Gogh, he thought, but also with that of other nineteenth-century artists, in either the permanent collection

Edouard Manet, Les courses (The Races), litho 1865/72

or in temporary exhibitions. It is with this brief in mind that the present volume intentionally surrounds the work of Vincent van Gogh with that of other artists displayed under the same roof in Amsterdam. The book thus seeks to acquaint the reader with the 'entourage d'amis et d'artistes' whose work the Van Gogh brothers personally admired, notwithstanding the second thoughts they had about some of them. The brothers' collection and indeed their legacy continues to evolve under the constant care of the Museum's staff. They draw inspiration from one of Vincent's own remarks in a letter he wrote Theo in January 1874: '*admire as many works of art* as you can, most people *don't admire enough*'.

Romanticism and Realism

Although the Van Gogh Museum also preserves more than a thousand drawings, sketchbook sheets, letter illustrations and prints by Vincent van Gogh and the artists of his century, the illustrations selected for this volume were limited to works in oil, pastel or watercolour.

All of the works illustrated form part of the permanent collection of the Van Gogh Museum, unless otherwise indicated, and are arranged in accordance with Van Gogh's biography. The first section sketches the cultural ambience of France and Holland at the moment when Vincent van Gogh was first introduced to art as a young dealer entering the service of the firm Goupil & Cie. The illustrations of the artist's works correspond to the various stages of his artistic

pilgrimage: the successive sojourns in The Hague, Drenthe, Nuenen, Antwerp, Paris, Arles, St-Rémy and Auvers-sur-Oise. The book also focuses on the artists with whom Van Gogh became acquainted during his Parisian period (1886-1887), whose influence triggered a revolution in his style. We conclude with a section about the work of several artists who are particularly representative of the period between 1890 and World War I.

Van Gogh's own works are often described through quotations from the artist's correspondence, just as many of the other painters in this volume are seen primarily through his eyes. Many of the texts accompanying the illustrations draw a connection between a given work and Vincent's estimation of the artist. The translated excerpts from the letters are based on the integral Dutch-language edition published by the Van Gogh Museum, De brieven van Vincent van Gogh (1990). So as not to encumber the text unnecessarily, the precise origins of these quotations is not indicated. However, the dates of the letters quoted, mostly to his brother Theo, are stated whenever possible, so that they can be traced without difficulty.

The inventory number of every work has been provided.

The significance of the various letters is as follows:

S: painting
D: drawing, watercolour or pastel
P: print
V: object or sculpture

M: property of the Van Gogh Museum
V: property of the Vincent van Gogh Foundation, on permanent loan to the Van Gogh Museum
B: on loan from museums or private individuals
F: the number assigned to the work in J.-B. de la Faille, The Works of Vincent van Gogh. His Paintings and Drawings, Amsterdam 1970

The year at the end of each inventory number indicates when the work entered the Museum, be it as a gift, a loan or a purchase.

Ary Scheffer
Dordrecht 1795-1858 Argenteuil
Christus Consolator
Canvas, 184 × 248 cm - 1837
Inv. S 10 B/1987, on loan from the Amsterdams
Historisch Museum (Fodor Collection)

It was not until 1880 that Vincent van Gogh abandoned his initial, religious vocation in favour of an artistic one. The experience he had gained as a shop assistant in London and Paris in the 1870s with the international art dealers Goupil & Cie would play a decisive role in the formation of his taste. This first chapter will take us into the world of the French, English and Dutch painters whose work the young Dutchman knew. Ary Scheffer's huge canvas of 1837 casts Christ as the Comforter of suffering mankind. From the early '70s until his Hague period, Van Gogh kept an engraving after this picture on the walls of his various flats. Indeed he saw the

work as a parable of his own experience. As he wrote his brother Theo from London in July 1876: 'I am bound in different ways, some even humiliating, and these will become even more confining in time; but the words written above *Christus Consolator* – "He has come to proclaim liberty to the captives" – hold true to this day'. The canvas contains an allusion to the Greek struggle for independence and shows a slave liberated from his shackles in the foreground. Van Gogh's appreciation for Scheffer cooled in the course of his career. He associated him with such artists as Delaroche and Gérôme, 'who are not really *painters*'.

Virgilio Narcisso Diaz de la Peña
Bordeau2 1808-1876 Menton
Nymph with Cupids
Canvas, 44 × 32.5 cm - 1851
Inv. S 23 B/1991, on loan from the Amsterdam
Historisch Museum (Fodor Collection)

occasionally populated with graceful nymphs. He also produced flower still lifes, mythological scenes and oriental subjects. His affluence enabled Diaz to support less fortunate colleagues, such as Jongkind, Millet and Rousseau. Van Gogh became familiar with the work of Diaz while working in the art trade in the 1870s. In the early '80s he saw still more of it in The Hague, both in temporary exhibitions and in the collection of the painter Hendrik Willem Mesdag. As a novice Van Gogh sought to imitate the Frenchman, from whom he learned 'the relative proportion of the planes and masses' and 'that colour expressed form'. After visiting the Fodor Collection in Amsterdam in October 1885, he wrote his brother 'Diaz is a *painter* to the marrow – and he is conscientious to his fingertips. By the way the Fodor Diaz is more like a sketch, but that may be exactly why for me, not having seen them for years, it was a real pleasure to see one again'.

Virgilio Narcisso Diaz de la Peña
Idyll
Panel, 38 × 55 cm - 1853
Inv. S 87 B/1991, on loan from the Rijksmuseum

Diaz had his first taste of success at the Paris Salon of 1834. From the moment he won a medal at the Salon of 1844, he had the wind at his back. Nor did the artist have any moral compunction about making the requisite concessions to the marketplace: he was content to work in several genres at once in order to boost sales.
From 1835 Diaz paid an annual visit to Barbizon, where he painted landscapes primarily after the example of Théodore Rousseau. His specialty was mysteriously illuminated sylvan scenes, which – depending on his patron's wishes – he

Alexandre Gabriel Decamps
Paris 1803-1860 Fontainebleau
A Shepherd with his Flock
Canvas, 79 × 115 cm - 1843
Inv. S 22 B/1991, on loan from the Amsterdams
Historisch Museum (Fodor Collection)

'Decamps's shepherd is really a master-piece', Van Gogh wrote his brother in October 1885. He had just been admiring the picture at the Museum Fodor in Amsterdam, where – along with Scheffer's *Christus Consolator* – it was one of the top pieces. Recalling Fodor's superb collection of early nineteenth-century Dutch and French art, Van Gogh sighed: 'the *original* people of that period 40 years ago, I'm always glad to see them'. Decamps had long been one of

Vincent's favourite painters. When he became disgruntled with the artistic accomplishments of his contemporaries, as he did from time to time, a feeling crept over him of 'nostalgia for Decamps's less orthodox manner of painting'. He associated the artist's loose, broad style with the sentiment Victor Hugo's *Les misérables* roused in him: 'one gets warm from such a book, as from pictures by Dupré and old Millets, or a few Decamps'.

Van Gogh considered Delacroix not only the greatest colourist of his day, but also one of the few nineteenth-century artists who managed to paint convincing religious pictures. In September 1889 he wrote his brother, 'Do you know why the pictures of Eugène Delacroix – the religious and historical pictures, the *Bark of Christ*, the *Pietà*, the *Crusaders* – are so gripping? Because before Eugène Delacroix did a *Gethsemane*, he first went to see for himself what an olive grove was'.

Van Gogh destroyed his own attempt at the theme of *The Agony in the Garden* because he felt he had still not studied the forms in nature adequately. When in the late 1880s his colleague Emile Bernard sent him a photograph of *his* interpretation of *The Agony in the Garden*, Van Gogh was dismissive. He thought a modern artist should be capable of conveying a sense of anxiety without immediately referring to the historical Gethsemane: 'But what about Delacroix, you'll say. Delacroix indeed, but then you'd have a lot more work to do [...]'.

Eugène Delacroix
Charenton-St-Maurice 1798-1863 Paris
The Agony in the Garden
Canvas, 32 × 42 cm - 1861
Inv. S 86 B/1991, on loan from the
Rijksmuseum

Honoré Daumier
Marseilles 1808-1879 Valmondois
The Reading
Panel, 27 × 35 cm - 1857
Inv. S 84 B/1991, on loan from the
Rijksmuseum

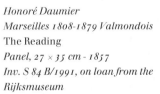

Daumier was famous for his many hundreds of satirical prints, which bespeak the artist's social *engagement*. Vincent developed a taste for his work at an early stage, and later decided 'he's of even greater importance than I thought'. Theo kept his brother well informed of Daumier's progress, but Vincent could not have actually seen many of the Frenchman's pictures. The physical characteristics of the people he saw around him during his stay in Provence in the late 1880s often reminded him of Daumier, and he intended to portray the postman Roulin 'in oils, off the cuff like Daumier'. Daumier was a master caricaturist. This talent is manifest in many of his paintings, even if they are generally less sarcastic and more reflective than his prints. The illustrated canvas dates from 1857, but the artist only sold it twenty years hence, when a certain Tabourier bought it for 1,200 francs. Daumier's oeuvre comprises more than one picture of people reading, a theme that likewise appealed to Van Gogh. *The Reader* by Meissonnier and *Portrait of Eugène Benon Reading* by Puvis de Chavannes were two of Vincent's favourite paintings.

On 18 February 1862 Millet wrote the following to the critic Théophile Thoré: 'In the "woman returning from the well" I've tried to make it so that she cannot be taken for either a water bearer or a servant; that she has just drawn water for the use of her household, water for making soup for her husband and his children; that she seems to be carrying no more nor less than the weight of the full pails; that through her sort of grimace, apparently forced by the weight pulling on her arms, and the squinting of her eyes, caused by the light, one senses an air of rustic goodness in her face. With a kind of horror I've eschewed, as always, anything that could be seen as sentimental'.

Van Gogh was deeply moved by Millet's remarks, which helped him define his artistic ideal of rural life. Millet's handling of the peasant genre constituted 'the very heart of modern art' in the Dutchman's eyes.

Alfred Sensier's 1881 biography of the French master became a veritable bible for Vincent, who believed that sincerity in life and art were inextricable. 'Father Millet' never ceased to be the autodidact's mentor. When he painted *The Potato Eaters* in Nuenen and later, when he tried his own hand at *The Sower* – the theme Millet had immortalised – the Frenchman was his standard for a kind of painting in which 'all reality [is] also a symbol'. In times of crisis, as in the asylum of St-Rémy, he managed to regain his composure by copying Millet.

This small picture of a *Girl Carrying Water* is a preparatory study for a work measuring one metre in height. In the 1880s, that canvas found its way into the Vanderbilt Collection in New York, as did Thomas Couture's *Le Réaliste*.

Jean-François Millet
Gruchy 1814-1875 Barbizon
Girl Carrying Water
Canvas, 41 × 33 cm - ca. 1855/56
Inv. S 93 B/1991, on loan from the
Rijksmuseum

Following Millet's death in 1875, the painters Jules Breton and Léon Lhermitte became the leading practitioners of the peasant genre, which they remained for the rest of the century.

As early as 1874 Van Gogh mentioned both Millet and Breton in a list of his favourite artists. He even made a pilgrimage to the latter's home in the village of Courrières. Van Gogh also admired the poetry of Breton, whom he called 'the voice of the corn'.

The girl in Breton's *Peasant Girl with Hoe* is seen resting after a day of hard work on the land, with the tower of the church of Courrières in the background. A few minor adjustments and she could easily serve as a personification of Melancholy. In his book on the Salon of 1888, published by the firm of Goupil, the critic Henry Houssaye noted Breton's tendency to classicise his peasant women, and indeed his phrase 'a modern Ceres' could well be applied to our picture. With its austere composition and sober palette, the work emanates a serenity far removed from the sort of sentimentality to which other practitioners of the peasant genre often succumbed.

Compared to Breton's unassuming canvas, Léon Lhermitte's monumental treatment of a small group of farm labourers taking a rest from their haymaking has all the earmarks of an ambitious showpiece. When Jules Bastien-Lepage died in 1884, Lhermitte became one of the foremost younger painters who specialised in country life. Though Lhermitte had long since made his debut at the Salon in 1864, Van Gogh only became aware of him in February 1883, upon reading an exhibition review that placed the artist on a par with Millet and Breton. No sooner did Van Gogh see some reproductions of his work a month later than Lhermitte became one of his heroes.

The Dutchman immediately recognised a painter who 'knows the sturdy, stern working man's figure through and through, and takes his subjects from the very heart of the people'. While Vincent was wrestling with *The Potato Eaters* in 1885 he drew inspiration from Lhermitte's working method, which he found similar to his own. Judging from such details as heads and hands, it became clear to him that 'artists such as Lhermitte must have studied the peasant figure not only from a distance, but also at close range. In a letter to his brother he even went so far as to compare Lhermitte to Rembrandt: 'He is the absolute master of the figure. He can do with it whatever he wants – proceeding neither from the colour nor from the local tone but rather from the light, as Rembrandt did. There is something astonishingly masterful in everything he does. He excelled above all at modelling, perfectly satisfying the demand for sincerity'.

In 1887 Lhermitte signed a contract with Theo van Gogh's firm Boussod & Valadon.

Jules Breton
Courrières 1827-1906 Paris
Peasant Girl with Hoe
Canvas, 51.5 × 46 cm - 1882
Inv. S 386 M/1988

Vincent must have seen *The Haymakers*
that year when it was exhibited at the
Salon. At the Exposition Universelle in
Paris in 1889, where *The Haymakers*
was again displayed, the artist was
crowned with the *grand prix*. The work
was also exhibited in America in 1891
and 1893, and then purchased for the
Buffalo Fine Arts Academy in New York.
For the Van Gogh Museum it was
acquired in 1991.

Léon Lhermitte
Mont-St-Père 1844-1925 Paris
The Haymakers (La fenaison)
Canvas, 215.9 × 264.2 cm - 1887
Inv. S 424 M/1991

Charles François Daubigny
Paris 1817-1878 Auvers-sur-Oise
Evening Landscape
Canvas, 28 × 60.5 cm - 1860
Inv. S 37 B/1991, on loan from the
Rijksdienst Beeldende Kunst

Charles François Daubigny
Landscape
Panel, 24.5 × 54.5 cm
Inv. S 82 B/1991, on loan from the Rijksmuseum

Daubigny's style is halfway between the Barbizon School and the Impressionists, whose work he promoted as a member of the jury of the Salon. In 1860 – the year *Evening Landscape* was painted – he settled in Auvers-sur-Oise. Thenceforth his reputation rested primarily on his evocations of the picturesque river landscapes he observed in the immediate surroundings of his house. These he usually recorded from a *bateau-atelier*, as Monet would do later on. He also made regular excursions to other parts of France; the second landscape can be traced to Brittany, near the village of Kerity.

When Van Gogh arrived in Auvers-sur-Oise in 1890, he discovered that Daubigny's widow was still living there. Having admired her husband for many years, he painted her garden in his honour.

Jean-Baptiste Corot
Paris 1796-1875 Paris
Souvenir of Les Landes
Canvas, 38 × 56.5 cm - ca. 1872
Inv. S 76 B/1991, on loan from the
Rijksmuseum

Only relatively late in life, in 1821, did Jean-Baptiste Corot, the son of a Parisian merchant, decide to devote his life to painting. He painted his first landscapes in the vicinity of Fontainebleau, in Normandy and on the Channel coast. In 1825 he went to Italy to finish his training, and in 1827 made his debut at the Paris Salon. Though his talent was quickly recognised, Corot preferred to remain aloof to the official art world. From 1849 he was on a friendly footing with several members of the Barbizon School, with which he came to be associated.

For the younger generation of landscape painters 'le Père Corot' became a mentor. In 1875, the year Corot died, Van Gogh visited the late artist's memorial exhibition in Paris and gleaned a good deal of personal information about him from the catalogue. As 'simple as a labourer', Corot bought bread every day from the local baker and then ate it in the field where he was working. What intrigued the Dutch artist most about Corot's painting was his use of colour – 'ce gris argent' – and his remarkable handling of light effects. Every time he saw the Frenchman's work he experienced the same sensation: 'a quiet, a calmness and a peace, which is enchanting'.

François Bonvin
Paris 1817-1887 St-Germain-en-Laye
Still Life with Drawing Paraphernalia
Zinc, 25 × 36.5 cm - 1879
Inv. S 431 M/1992

Each in its own fashion, these two pictures comment on the artistic life of the nineteenth century. Couture satirised Realism in contemporary painting while Bonvin, a Realist to the bone, depicted the objects most familiar to an artist – drawing paraphernalia – for his sensitive still life, which was originally accompanied by a picture of painting appurtenances.

Couture's satire on Realism dates from 1865, when established artists were worried about the movement's ascent. Though Couture's own art was far from academic, he condemned the 'banality' of Realism as opposed to the sort of poetic painting he championed. Gustave Courbet was his *bête noire;* indeed the illustrated canvas ridicules the very principles sacred to Courbet, Daumier and later also Van Gogh. It shows an artist in his studio, painting the animal traditionally associated with stupidity, the swine. On the wall hang commonplace, insignificant objects. The bottle in the foreground suggests the artist was no stranger to the pleasures of the grape. Nor does he scruple to use the head of Olympian Zeus as a seat.

Interestingly enough, Couture's *Realist* belonged to the renowned Vanderbilt Collection in New York in the nineteenth century.

Thomas Couture
Senlis 1815-1879 Villiers-le-Bel
The Realist (Le Réaliste)
Canvas, 46 × 38 cm - 1865
Inv. S 387 M/1987
Acquired with the support of the
Vereniging Rembrandt

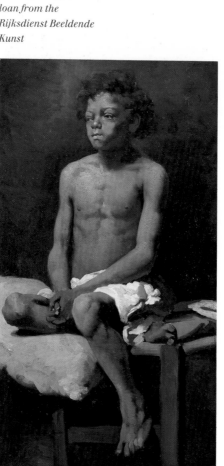

Matthijs Maris painted this figure study of a small boy at the academy in Antwerp, where he preceded Van Gogh by some thirty years. Many Dutch artists chose to study in the Flemish city, partly because there was no tuition fee. Whereas many of his fellow students preferred painting oriental or Italian models from life, Van Gogh insisted on finding his models on the street. As he wrote his brother in July 1885, 'Nothing seems simpler than painting peasants, ragpickers and other kinds of labourers, but – no subjects in painting are as difficult as these commonplace figures! As far as I know there isn't a single academy where one learns to draw and paint a digger, a sower, a woman hanging a kettle over the fire or a seamstress'. In the same letter the artist reflected on the difficulty of capturing the working class actually at work. He saw it as a new challenge for contemporary artists, for 'even the figures of [the seventeenth-century Dutch artists] Ostade and Ter Borch don't work as people do nowadays. [...] Did they ever attempt to make "a labourer"? Did Velàzquez try it in his water carrier or in his common types? No. *Work*, that's something the figures in the old pictures don't do'. Van Gogh's comments notwithstanding, it was none other than seventeenth-century Spanish painters on whom Théodule Ribot modelled his depictions of working-class occupations. The work

of masters such as Velàzquez and Ribera was displayed in a 'galerie espagnole' in the Louvre, which had recently been opened by King Louis Philippe. The same pictures also inspired Ribot's friend Manet.
At first Ribot's career proceeded by fits and starts. Yet from the moment he made his debut at the Salon with pictures of kitchen boys, he had no difficulty selling his tonal genre paintings and still lifes. His colleagues honoured him with a dinner in 1884. In the presence of, among others, Fantin-Latour, Bastien-Lepage, Raffaëlli and Monet, he received a medal in recognition of his stature as a 'peintre indépendant'.

These pendants, showing a manservant and a housekeeper respectively, illustrate Carolus Duran's early advocacy of Courbet's particular brand of Realism. He was one of the artists in Manet's circle at the time of the Salon des Refusés in 1863, and taught young Berthe Morisot how to paint. On a visit to Spain in 1868 he became fascinated with the art of Velàzquez. Carolus Duran's portrait of his wife, *La Dame au gant*, painted following his return to France, betrayed his indebtedness to the Spanish master, and established him as a society painter. Van Gogh admired the portrait in the Musée du Luxembourg; it was one of 'those not very serious things that I find very beautiful', he wrote, adding that 'if a painter makes what he sees, he'll always be someone'. Carolus Duran's sophisticated, restrained palette and Whistler-like chic distinguished him from more frivolous colleagues such as Alexandre Cabanel.

Emile Charles Carolus Duran
Lille 1837-1917 Paris
The Manservant
Panel, 59 × 18.5 cm - 1861. Inv. S 26 B/1991,
on loan from the Rijksmuseum Kröller-Müller

Emile Charles Carolus Duran
The Housekeeper
Panel, 59 × 18.5 cm - 1861.
Inv. S 25 B/1991,
on loan from the Rijksmuseum Kröller-Müller

Gustave Courbet
Ornans 1819-1877 La Tour de Peilz
Still Life with Apples
Canvas, 59 × 48 cm - 1872
Inv. S 79 B/1991, on loan from the Rijksmuseum

Courbet is the pre-eminent exponent of the revolutionary Realism that dominated French painting in the mid-nineteenth century. He created quite a stir with such manifesto-like pictures as *A Funeral at Ornans* and *The Stone-breakers* and offended contemporary sensibilities with his provocative portrayals of women. In 1871 he was imprisoned for six months for his alleged role in pulling down the column on the Place Vendôme during the revolt of the Paris Commune. While confined in the prison of Sainte-Pélagie he made several still lifes with apples. The vigour of these works has been seen as a token of Courbet's indomitable spirit during his incarceration.

Compared with that of Millet, Courbet's name is rarely mentioned in Van Gogh's correspondence. As a resolute realist, the Dutchman affirmed Courbet's famous statement that having never seen angels, he could not paint them. Ultimately, however, Vincent felt more affinity with Millet's humanitarian vision of mankind than with Courbet's more aggressive approach. He seems to have admired the former's portraits, nudes and landscapes most of all. Together with Manet, Van Gogh believed Courbet had all but resolved the classical dilemma, that is, how to make 'form and colour go together'.

Pierre Puvis de Chavannes
Lyons 1824-1898 Paris
Still Life with Fruit and Flowers
Canvas, 44.5 × 59.5 cm - ca. 1870
Inv. S 414 M/1990

Despite the many official commissions he received, Puvis de Chavannes long remained a controversial artist. Not until the 1880s, almost from one day to the next, did he become a cult figure for the young Symbolists and Neo-impressionists. His *L'Espérance* and *Le Pauvre Pêcheur* (now both in the Musée d'Orsay) were admired by Paul Gauguin and Georges Seurat, and Vincent van Gogh was also influenced by him. Puvis's *Portrait of Eugène Benon* – the same Benon to whom the artist dedicated this still life – even inspired two of the Dutch painter's canvases: *Romans parisiens* (1887) and the *Portrait of Dr Gachet* (1890).

Puvis de Chavannes is frequently quoted as saying 'I have always tried to say as much as possible in as few words as possible'. Our austere still life aptly illustrates this statement. It is one of the few examples of the genre in his oeuvre, most of which are no more than detail studies for larger works. Though the tone and composition bear super-ficial resemblance to still lifes by Fantin-Latour, the fruit and the small bouquet are less imposing or eager to please. Their arrangement on the white damask is every bit as severe and impressive as the allegorical figures in Puvis's monumental decorations.

Pierre Puvis de Chavannes, Lyons 1824-1898 Paris
St Geneviève as a Child in Prayer
Paper on canvas, 136.5 × 76.2 cm - ca. 1874-76, inv. S 438 M/1993
Acquired with the support of the Vereniging Rembrandt, the Vincent van
Gogh Foundation and the Ministry of Welfare, Public Health and Culture

Puvis de Chavannes studied briefly under such diverse teachers as Thomas Couture, Eugène Delacroix and Henri Scheffer. At an early stage he was given the opportunity to paint a decorative ensemble for the house of his brother in the town of Brouchy. With that he discovered his vocation, and after the French State purchased his *Concordia* at the Salon of 1861, monumental commissions for Amiens and Marseilles followed.

Puvis de Chavannes is considered the most important innovator in the field of nineteenth-century monumental painting. While many of his contemporaries delighted in crowding their historical works with archeological detail, Puvis abhorred superfluity and strove for simple, abstracted compositions characterised by large fields of colour and a restrained palette. Under the influence of such Renaissance artists as Giotto and Piero della Francesca, Puvis made numerous preparatory studies for his figures, progressively abstracting them in a lengthy reductive process. His chalky manner of painting, which is intentionally primitivistic, lends his compositions a serene, timeless quality.

In 1874 Philippe de Chennevières, director of the Beaux-Arts, commissioned Puvis, along with eleven other artists, to decorate the Panthéon. The structure had been built as a church under Louis XV and dedicated to the patroness of Paris, St Geneviève. The decoration was intended to illustrate the life of the Saint, and Puvis was asked to visualise her youth ('la vie pastorale de la jeune sainte').

Born in the year 422, the historical St Geneviève spent her youth tending her father's sheep in the foothills of Mont Valérien. Not only did she success-fully defend the Gauls against the incursions of the Huns, but also she was endowed with the gift of healing. Puvis's murals show the worthy maiden in an Arcadian landscape, kneeling in prayer while a Gallic couple and a child look on. The inscription beneath the composition explains the scene: 'From her earliest youth St Geneviève displayed intense piety; praying constantly she surprised and amazed everyone who saw her'. Calling the composition a prologue to the entire cycle, Puvis described it as follows: 'I have had the small Saint *appear* to a rustic couple, a woodcutter and his wife with their child [...].

In order to avoid excessive verisimilitude and to enhance the emotional effect, I also meant the form and costume of the praying child to seem more angelic than human, more visionary than realistic; the aureole encircling her head completes the illusion. That is how she appears to the naïve, bewildered couple'.

The Parisian public already had the opportunity to admire the prayerful Geneviève at the Salon of 1876, before the canvas – measuring 4.62 x 2.21 metres – was installed in the Panthéon in May 1877.

After finishing a mural Puvis often executed replicas of it. The Fogg Art Museum in Cambridge, Massachusetts preserves a replica from 1879, for instance, of the same format as the composition shown here. Yet our version is a preparatory study in oil, presumably painted between 1874 and 1876, which the artist presented 'affectueusement' to Count Joseph Primoli. The definitive work deviates only superficially from this design: in the Panthéon, Puvis merely altered the decorative garlands bordering the composition.

This sketch by Puvis de Chavannes shows a classical figure absorbed in his book. The olive-green background would have appealed to Van Gogh, for in his opinion Puvis was better suited than any other artist 'to explain olive trees' to mankind.

Vincent's last letters from Auvers contain rapturous passages about the art of Puvis, which he considered nothing less than a 'beneficent renascence of everything you've believed in, what you've longed for, a curious encounter between remote Antiquity and the coarse modern age'. We cannot know exactly how much Puvis influenced Van Gogh, or how much more he would have done so, had the Dutch artist lived longer. Vincent was convinced the coming generation would attach the same importance to

Puvis – 'a boundless talent who will always be a source of consolation' – as he did to Delacroix and Millet. And indeed, toward the end of his life, Puvis did begin to attract a growing number of followers. When he visited the Salon of 1896 the writer Emile Zola was even somewhat alarmed at the extent to which a new generation of painters had managed to derail both Impressionism and Symbolism: the exhibition was littered with all sorts of mystical pictures. 'I am afraid that the very great and very pure artist Puvis de Chavannes is responsible for this', wrote Zola. 'His disciples are a disaster, possibly even more disastrous than those of Manet, Monet and Pissarro'.

Pierre Puvis de Chavannes
The Reader
(Le Liseur)
Oil on prepared paper on canvas
55.6 × 46.1 cm
Inv. S 428 M/1992

Lourens Alma Tadema
Dronrijp 1836-1912 Wiesbaden
Portrait of George Henschel
Panel, 48.9 × 34.9 cm - 1879
Inv. S 426 M/1991

native Holland, where his friends included the painter Hendrik Willem Mesdag and the writer Carel Vosmaer. Few realise that Alma Tadema was also an outstanding portraitist, as evidenced by the more than seventy portraits he left. Those of his fellow artists are often penetrating. He painted striking likenesses of the sculptor Jules Dalou and his family in 1876 (Musée d'Orsay) and the painter Alfred Waterhouse in 1891. There were also many musicians among his sitters, such as the conductor Hans Richter (1881), the Polish piano virtuoso Ignacy Jan Paderewski (1891), and the composer-violinist Joseph Joachim (1893). Indeed there was always music at the Alma Tademas' house in London: besides those previously mentioned, composers such as Boito, Bruch, Saint-Saëns, Sarasate, Clara Schumann and Tchaikovsky performed there, and Nellie Melba and Caruso sang. In 1879 the Silesian singer George Henschel (1850-1934) likewise sat for the artist; the portrait shows the baritone accompanying himself on the handsome piano Alma Tadema kept in his studio. In 1928 Henschel made several recordings of himself singing lieder by Schubert and Schumann, much the same repertoire we know was performed during the musical evenings at the house of the Dutchman. As both a singer and conductor, Henschel played a prominent role in British musical life for many years, and was knighted by George V in 1914.

Of Dutch origins, Alma Tadema studied in Antwerp, where he overlapped with the brothers Jacob and Matthijs Maris. From 1864 he worked in Paris, where he spent some time in Gérôme's studio. The Franco-Prussian War drove him to London, where he had previously enjoyed several years of success and where he now settled once and for all.

Alma Tadema's growing reputation eventually won official recognition, and he was knighted Sir Lawrence Alma Tadema. His polished genre scenes visualising daily life in ancient Rome were renowned, even if his detractors claimed the marble in his pictures had more warmth than the figures. Alma Tadema never lost contact with his

George Henry Boughton
Norwich 1833-1905 London
God Speed! Pilgrims Setting Out for Canterbury
Canvas, 122 × 184 cm - 1874
Inv. S 380 M/1986

As a young man, Vincent van Gogh did not much care for English art. 'It takes some getting used to', he wrote his brother from London in July 1873. To his way of thinking, Victorian artists lacked a certain feeling for what he considered real painting, the same feeling that had been so characteristic of their forerunners Constable and Turner. He did find some 'clever painters' in England nonetheless, and in January 1874 added Boughton to his list of favourites. This admirable canvas, illustrating an episode from Chaucer's *Canterbury Tales*, was

acquired by the Museum in 1986. In the nineteenth century it was enthusiastically received at both the annual exhibition of London's Royal Academy in 1874 and the International Exhibition in Philadelphia in 1876. Van Gogh became so enamoured of the work in London that, in 1876, as a lay preacher at the Methodist church in Richmond, he worked Boughton's picture, as well as John Bunyan's popular book *Pilgrim's Progress*, into a sermon, which likened life to a pilgrimage en route to God. In fact when he chanced to see the older artist

in London he could not bring himself to address him, since he 'felt so much respect in his presence'. Boughton was one of those 'who seek true simplicity', like Millet, Israëls and Breton. In the early '80s Van Gogh copied Boughton's figures, pinned reproductions of his work to the wall and studied his woodcuts. Indeed, until the end of his Nuenen period his correspondence leaves no doubt that he deeply admired the English artist.

Charles Prévost
Spanish Woman with
Dog
Canvas, 46 × 35 cm
Inv. S 279 V/1962

Alfred Stevens
Brussels 1828-1906 Paris
Young Woman before a Mirror
Canvas, 126 × 67 cm
Inv. S 68 B/1991, on loan from the
Rijksdienst Beeldende Kunst

From the latter half of the 1850s the Belgian painter Alfred Stevens, who studied under the Neo-classical artists Ingres and Navez, won success in Paris with his portrayals of the 'modern woman'. He was also one of the first to succumb to the charm of Japonism. It may seem surprising that Van Gogh, who was so enamoured of peasant life, admired an artist like Stevens. Yet in early May 1885 he opined that 'it all depends on how much life and passion an artist can give his figure; if it's really alive, then a female figure by Alfred Stevens, for instance, or some of Tissot's, can also be really superb'. *Spanish Woman with Dog*, by the relatively unknown painter Prévost, hung on the wall of Theo van Gogh's apartment in Paris. His brother Vincent admired the wide range of greys, which he saw as 'pure Velàsquez'. These canvases give us a glimpse of the comfortable world of fashionable women in the latter half of the nineteenth century.

Alfred Stevens
L'Inde à Paris: the Exotic Bibelot
Canvas, 73.7 × 59.7 cm - ca. 1867
Inv. S 439 M/1993

This richly upholstered interior with a young woman lost in her 'rêve d'Orient' attests to Alfred Stevens's predilection for oriental *objets d'art*. Along with Félix Bracquemond, James McNeil Whistler, Edouard Manet and the brothers Goncourt, the Belgian artist was one of the first exponents of Japonism. The objects illustrated here – a Japanese lacquered screen, an oriental carpet and a pouf, and the rather curious elephant set with jewels – all belonged to Stevens's own collection and are also found in other paintings by him.

The most striking object is the elephant, the 'bibelot exotique' mentioned in the title. Still in the possession of the artist's descendants, it is also found in a homonymous painting of the same period. The seemingly Japanese doll does not figure in the other picture, however, and would hardly have belonged to this Indian elephant originally.

There are three pictures by Stevens with the same title, one of which the artist showed at the Exposition Universelle of 1867, along with no less than seventeen other works. He won a first-class medal for his efforts, and was awarded the Légion d'Honneur. That Stevens's reputation survived the rest of the century can be deduced from the fact that our picture was displayed at the Exposition Universelle of 1900. One of the reviewers of the exhibition of 1867, Camille Lemonnier, regarded *L'Inde à Paris* as symptomatic of an aesthetic revolution that had just taken place: 'a new ideal appears with this exotic art, a grandiose jewel set with carbuncles, which suddenly appears at the borders of the west; and the daydreaming Parisienne [...], who with her pearly eyes seems to drink in the beauty of the enigmatic object, visualises perfectly the passionate curiosity that has captured everyone's soul'.

Before the Van Gogh Museum purchased it in 1993 as an early example of Japonism in nineteenth-century art, the picture had belonged to various American and European collections, including that of the Parisian art dealers Boussod, Valadon & Cie.

Philippe Rousseau
Paris 1816-1887 Acquigny
Still Life
Canvas, 98 × 130.5 cm
Inv. S 66 B/1991, on loan from the
Rijksdienst Beeldende Kunst

During a brief sojourn in Amsterdam in October 1885 Van Gogh visited the recently opened Rijksmuseum, where a number of still lifes caught his attention. As one would expect, his taste ran to 'simple' examples of the genre, to which he attached 'much more artistic value than to many pretentious canvases'. On that occasion he wondered what the De Goncourt brothers had written about Jean-Siméon Chardin (1699-1779), the pre-eminent painter of austere still lifes, in their book on the eighteenth century. Four years later, writing to his brother from St-Rémy, Vincent posed the following question: 'When the object represented is, in point of style, in complete harmony and at one with the manner of representing it, isn't that exactly what gives a work of art its quality? That's why, as far as painting goes, an ordinary loaf of bread is an especially good motif when it's painted by Chardin!' On another occasion he wrote that what made a work of art 'Chardin-esque' was 'a peculiar expression of *simplicity* and *goodness* – both *through and through*'.

Philippe Rousseau
Still Life with Game
Canvas, 115.5 ×
88.5 cm - 1887
Inv. S 441 M/1993
Presented by the
Friends of the
Van Gogh Museum

Though Van Gogh executed over 160 still lifes in the course of his short career, the still life painters of his own day rarely figure in his correspondence. Philippe Rousseau may have been hailed by his contemporaries as the 'Chardin of the nineteenth century', for instance, but is not even mentioned by Vincent.

Rousseau was active during the Second Empire. His clients included Emperor Napoleon III and his court as well as James baron de Rothschild. The writer and critic Théophile Gautier hailed Rousseau as a full-blooded Realist and even the discriminating Baudelaire spoke of his work in glowing terms. The largest of these three still lifes, with its assemblage of objects and fruit, exemplifies Rousseau at his most ambitious and extravagant. Generally, however, he preferred more modest subjects. Not only did he imitate Chardin's pastel technique and subtle rendering of texture, but he also depicted many of the same objects, such as the peaches in the pastel or the lifeless animals in the *Still Life with Game*. He borrowed the silver beaker that appears in these last two works from Chardin's *Le gobelet d'argent* in the Louvre. The same decorative object is found in still lifes by Rousseau's colleague and friend Bonvin.

Philippe Rousseau
Pêches au vin
Pastel, 73 × 92 cm
Inv. D 1008 M/1990

Ignace Henri Fantin-Latour
Grenoble 1836-1904 Buré
Still Life with a Basket of Grapes and an Apple
Canvas, 32 × 40.5 cm - 1890
Inv. S 16 B/1990, private collection

François Bonvin specialised in humble subjects. Besides intimate still lifes he also painted numerous genre scenes populated by members of the working class. Bonvin moved in the circle of the Realist Courbet; when a number of young Realists were denied admission to the Salon in 1859, he let his colleagues Fantin-Latour, Whistler and Ribot exhibit their work in his studio. Besides Chardin, Bonvin was also influenced by the seventeenth-century Dutch still lifes he had seen in the Louvre and in Holland itself, which he visited in 1867. Though as a genre, still life was not highly regarded by the Salon, Bonvin won several medals and the Légion d'honneur was conferred on him in 1870.

François Bonvin
Paris 1817-1887 St-Germain-en-Laye
Still Life
Canvas, 45.5 × 36 cm - 1871, inv. S 74 B/1991,
on loan from the Rijksmuseum

Fantin-Latour was closely associated with the first generation of Impressionists, a number of whom he represented in group portraits. Though his lack of stylistic daring relative to his confrères did nothing to help his reputation, he became famous as a painter of still lifes – something he himself found rather ironic since he gained little satisfaction from the genre. As his friend and colleague Whistler pointed out, his still lifes were essentially colour studies. Never routine or cliché, the palette and composition of his flower pieces are always inventive and unconventional.

Ignace Henri Fantin-Latour
Still Life with Flowers
Canvas, 54 × 60.5 cm - 1877
Inv. S 219 V/1962

Vincent considered flowers an
eminently suitable motif for colour
research while he was living in Paris.
Judging from one of the letters he
penned during his Brabant period, he
hardly knew the Frenchman's work at
that time, but what he had seen he
described as 'Chardin-esque, and that's
saying a lot'.
He particularly admired painters who
went about blazing their own trails
without a great deal of fanfare. As he
wrote Emile Bernard in the autumn of
1887, 'Well then, that's someone
[Fantin] who hasn't rebelled.
And does that prevent him from having
that indefinable calm and that right-
eousness which makes him one of the
most independent minds of our day?'
The 1877 still life by Fantin-Latour was
acquired by Jo van Gogh in April 1909.
She got it from the art dealer C.M. van
Gogh in exchange for Vincent van Gogh's
*Portrait of a Girl Holding a Bunch of
Flowers*, the famous *La Mousmé* from
Arles.

For Jacob Maris – the elder brother of Matthijs and later the leading member of the Hague School – Jean-Baptiste Corot was a pole star during the Dutchman's Parisian period (1865-1871). In this view of the village of Montigny-sur-Loing, situated on a tributary of the Seine, Corot's influence, like that of Daubigny, is evident.

In a letter written in October 1888 Van Gogh characterised the work Jacob Maris produced after returning to Holland as 'heavy'. Painted while Maris was still living in France, the present canvas could hardly be described as such. On the contrary, this convincing synthesis of Vincent's favourites Daubigny and Corot would have pleasantly surprised the Dutchman.

Jacob Maris
The Hague 1837-1899 Karlsbad
View of Montigny-sur-Loing
Canvas, 20.5 × 30.5 cm - 1869
Inv. S 389 M/1989

Carl Schuch
Vienna 1846-1903
Vienna
By the Woods
Canvas, 68 × 54 cm
Inv. S 67 B/1991
on loan from the
Rijksdienst Beeldende
Kunst

Carl Schuch belonged to the circle of Wilhelm Leibl and Wilhelm Trübner, who introduced Courbet's Realism to Germany. After travelling throughout Italy, Schuch subsequently worked for some time in Paris. In the early 1890s mental illness compelled him to lay down his brush. He spent the period from 1894 until his death in a sanatorium.

Though as a painter Schuch was noted primarily for his subtle still lifes, he also produced some memorable landscapes. During the summer of 1872 he made landscape studies in the Viennese suburb of Purkersdorf. The following year he visited the Meyer Collection in Dresden, where he became acquainted with works by Corot, Daubigny and Théodore Rousseau. Our forest view probably originated during this period. In his own eyes, most of Schuch's landscape paintings were merely studies preparatory to an 'ideal' masterpiece the Austrian artist never realised.

Compared to his fellow members of the Hague School Matthijs Maris was a maverick. His work recalls late Romantic German illustrators such as Richter and Rethel, the English Pre-Raphaelites and Monticelli. In the final analysis, however, it is unique. Though at first he enjoyed some measure of success, Maris eventually became isolated both socially and artistically. From May 1869 Matthijs Maris lived with his brother Jacob in Paris. Jacob eventually returned to Holland but Matthijs stayed on in penury. In 1875, the year *Girl with Goats* was painted, the young Vincent van Gogh met the eccentric artist in the French capital and even compiled a poetry album for him, transcribing poems by Goethe, Heine and Andersen. Maris's uncompromising dedication to his work deeply inspired Van Gogh. Years later, in May 1885, he could still not accept Maris's lot: 'If they hadn't made Thijs Maris too wretched and too melancholy to work, perhaps he would have found something surprising. I think of that fellow so often, Theo, because his work is so marvellous. It's the work of a dreamer – but what an artist! By God, if that fellow were now what he was when he began!'

Matthijs Maris
The Hague 1839-1917 London
Girl with Goats
Canvas, 65.1 × 101.4 cm - 1875
Inv. S 412 M/1990

Among the painters of the Hague School, Weissenbruch and Mauve excelled as watercolourists. Mauve, who lived in The Hague from 1874, could perfectly capture the silvery atmosphere of beaches and dunes. Most of his landscapes are animated with people at work, in this case a woman laying her wash out to dry on a bleaching field. In 1876, together with Willem Maris and Hendrik Mesdag, Mauve founded the 'Hollandsche Teekenmaatschappij' in The Hague, where the painters of the Hague School regularly exhibited their watercolours.

In late 1881 and early 1882, Mauve gave Vincent van Gogh, his cousin by marriage, several weeks' worth of drawing and painting lessons. The two men had difficulty getting on, however, and it was not long before they had a falling out. Shortly thereafter, in June 1882, Mauve worked for the first time in the town of Laren, in the area near Amsterdam known as the 'Gooi'. As the Gooi was still virtually untouched by

modern life, he decided to settle there in 1885. Vincent had moved to Arles in the meantime; when he learned of Mauve's unexpected death in 1888, he sent the artist's widow – his cousin Jet Carbentus – a 'souvenir de Mauve', being a picture with a blossoming peach tree.

In contrast to Mauve, the figures in Weissenbruch's landscapes are relatively insignificant, if indeed there

Johannes Hendrik Weissenbruch
The Hague 1824-1903 The Hague
Landscape with Windmills
Watercolour, 37 × 54 cm
Inv. D 07 B/1986, on loan from the
Rijksdienst Beeldende Kunst

———————————

———————————

Anton Mauve
Zaandam 1838-1888 Arnhem
Bleaching Field
Watercolour, 28 × 45.5 cm
Inv. D 779 M/1980

are any figures at all. It was nature itself on which the artist focused, more specifically a heavy downpour in this case. He found the natural world most beautiful in stormy weather, blanketed by cloudy skies: 'The sky in a picture, that's really something! The main thing! Sky and light are the great wizards. The sky determines the picture. Painters can never spend enough time looking at the sky. We depend on it. We thrive on rain and sunshine and pass through the arid showers [...]. One must see nature in action'. Van Gogh was familiar with Weissenbruch's work by 1872, and met the artist for the first time a year later. During the former's Hague period the

two men saw a good deal of one another, and indeed Weissenbruch was one of the few who demonstrated real understanding of Van Gogh's draughtsmanship. 'You just keep going, and when you're old you'll still look peacefully at your first studies'. Weissenbruch's was nothing if not a long career. His active life stretched all the way from the so-called 'romantic' generation to the Hague School. In 1847 he showed his work for the first time at the 'Levende Meesters' (Contemporary Masters) exhibition and began selling to museums early on. In 1866 he joined the Société Belge des Aquarellistes in Brussels. And in 1900, only three years

before his death, he visited Barbizon.

Jules van de Sande Bakhuyzen specialised in Drenthe landscapes. Van Gogh knew Bakhuyzen from as early as 1874, and was also in touch with him, while living in The Hague later on. Judging from the work Vincent produced in Drenthe in 1883 he had Bakhuyzen in mind, whom he saw as the upholder of traditional landscape painting in the face of every trend.

Of all the artists of the Hague School, Jozef Israëls was the one Van Gogh most admired. As early as January 1874 he listed him as one of the 'painters of whom I'm especially fond'. As a figure painter who specialised in peasants and fishermen, Israëls distinguished himself from most other members of the Hague School, who were primarily landscapists.

For a long time Israëls's dramatic scene from the life of a fisherman – *By Mother's Grave* (1856) – was Van Gogh's favourite painting. He was particularly enamoured of its 'Delacroix-like' technique. Yet to Vincent's way of thinking, Israëls was the Dutch equivalent not of Delacroix but of Millet, and he often mentioned both their names in the same breath. The greater sentimentality of Israëls's work has more in common with Victorian painting, however; it is not surprising that his clientèle included a great many collectors from England and Scotland. The influence of Israëls's scenes with fishermen is clearly perceptible in Van Gogh's Hague and Nuenen work. Vincent admired Israëls's monumental watercolour *Sewing School at Katwijk* at an exhibition organised by the Hollandsche Teekenmaatschappij in late summer 1881: 'a superb drawing by Israëls, [showing a] sewing school at Katwijk'. The theme's appeal to the younger artist is confirmed by the studies of fisherwomen from the village of Scheveningen that he made shortly thereafter. He hoped the motif – 'so incredibly beautiful' – would enable him to sell his first watercolour. Van Gogh would borrow yet another

theme from Israëls later on: an interior with a peasant family at table. The older artist's handling of this subject formed an early inspiration for Vincent's *Potato Eaters. Peasant Family at Table* was one of the works submitted to the Paris Salon of 1882, which subsequently found its way into an English collection. It is based on a series of drawings the artist made earlier that year in the Dutch village of Dongen. Van Gogh saw the canvas at Goupil's branch in The Hague, shortly before it was sent to Paris, and referred to it in a letter to his brother in March 1882: 'a small [Israëls] with, I would say, five or six figures, a peasant family seated at table'. In 1884 Goupil's reproduced a drawing after the painting in a portfolio entitled *Les grands peintres français et étrangers*.

Vincent van Gogh
Zundert 1853-1890 Auvers-sur-Oise
Scheveningen Woman Knitting
Watercolour, 23.3 × 9.7 cm - 1881
Inv. D 276 V/1969 - F871

Jozef Israëls
Sewing Class at Katwijk
Watercolour, 52 × 69.5 cm - 1881
Inv. D 913 M/1989

Anthon van Rappard
Zeist 1858-1892 Santpoort
Drenthe Peasant Woman
Canvas, 90 × 50.5 cm - 1882/1883
Inv. S 353 M/1974

Van Gogh in The Hague and Drenthe

In late December 1881 Van Gogh moved into a small flat just off The Hague's Schenkweg, 'about ten minutes behind Mauve'. He expected a great deal from the lessons he was to get from his cousin Anton Mauve and from his contact with the younger members of the Hague School. However things did not go according to plan. Mauve was very helpful at first, but the two artists tended to get on each other's nerves. Nor did Vincent's liaison with the pregnant prostitute Sien Hoornik do anything to improve his choleric cousin's opinion of him. H.G. Tersteeg, the influential art dealer who managed Goupil's branch in The Hague, turned against the novice as well. In the end the cousins parted ways. It was while he was still under Mauve's tutelage that Vincent painted his first picture, *Still Life with Cabbage and Clogs*. Yet most of his time in The Hague was spent drawing. His uncle, the art dealer C.M. van Gogh, gave the aspirant his first commission: twelve views of The Hague in pen and ink. A series of lithographs inspired by the 'Heads of the People', he had seen in the English magazine *The Graphic*, was undertaken but never finished.

When his relationship with Sien finally deteriorated and his finances showed no sign of improvement, Vincent decided to move to the Dutch province of Drenthe in the northeastern part of the country. He later avowed that he had taken this rather 'hasty' decision in the hope of finding 'something of the strict poetry of the real moors'. His colleague Anthon van Rappard had worked in the region previously, and on 13 August 1882, long before his departure for the province, Van Gogh wrote him about it: 'What you said about Drenthe interests me. I know absolutely nothing about it personally, but only what Mauve and Termeulen, among others, brought with them. I imagine it being like North Brabant *when I was young*, about 20 years ago [...]'. Having concentrated on urban themes while living in The Hague, Van Gogh reverted to landscapes and country life in Drenthe. Judging from the twenty-two letters he sent Theo from the province, he was terribly lonely. It had apparently pained him to leave Sien behind in The Hague. 'Theo, when I see such a poor woman on the heath with a child on her arm or at her breast, my eyes get moist. I'm reminded of her; her weakness and untidiness only make the likeness greater'. By early December the solitude had become too much for him: '*that* loneliness, encountered by a painter who in the middle of nowhere is taken by every Tom, Dick and Harry for a madman, murderer, vagabond, etc. etc.' He decided to return to Brabant, to live with his parents in Nuenen.

Vincent van Gogh
Still Life with Cabbage and Clogs
Oil on paper on panel, 34.5 × 55 cm -
December 1881
Inv. S 137 V/1962 - F 1

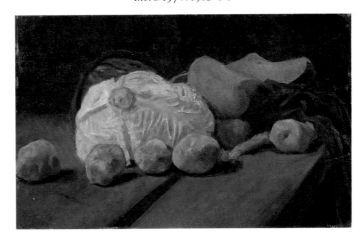

Vincent van Gogh
State Lottery Office
Watercolour, 38 × 57 cm - autumn 1882
Inv. D 376 V/1962 - F970

Vincent van Gogh
Bench with Four People
Watercolour (letter sketch), 9.4 × 11.7 cm - September 1882
Inv. D 321 V/1972

During the month of September 1882 Van Gogh occasionally attempted to produce a 'saleable' watercolour. The letter sketch with four locals sitting on a bench under a tree in The Hague is an example of these. Several weeks later he wrote Theo about it: 'Recently I've been painting almost nothing but watercolours. [...] Perhaps you remember Moorman's State Lottery Office at the top of Spuistraat? I passed by one rainy morning when a crowd of people were waiting to buy tickets. [...] I was struck by their expressions of anticipation and as I was working, they took on a greater, deeper significance than they had had at first. [The subject] becomes more meaningful, I think, if one interprets it as *the poor and money*'.

Vincent van Gogh
Beach at Scheveningen
Canvas, 34.5 × 51 cm - 1882
Inv. S 416 M/1990 - F 4

Marine and beach views have always been popular motifs in Dutch painting. Following the great florescence of the genre in the seventeenth century, the sea's beauty was rediscovered in the early nineteenth. In their turn, painters of the Hague School such as Jacob Maris, Hendrik Willem Mesdag and J.H. Weissenbruch upheld this tradition. The picturesque fishing village of Scheveningen was only a stone's throw from The Hague, and some artists chose to live within easy reach of the beach. Indeed Van Gogh's flat just off the Schenkweg was within minutes of it. His colleague Bernard Blommers let him store his materials in his studio in Scheveningen. This beach view is one of the first paintings Van Gogh ever made, and he was pleasantly surprised by the results. 'I thought the first things would look like nothing', he confessed.

No more than the members of the Hague School did he object to working outdoors in bad weather. The beach view was captured shortly before 'an angry storm', when the sea was the colour of 'dirty dishwater'.

Vincent van Gogh
Landscape in Drenthe with Canal and Sailboat
Pencil, pen, ink, heightened with white,
31.2 × 42.3 cm - autumn 1883
Inv. D 810 M/1986 - F 1104
Acquired with the support of the Vereniging
Rembrandt

'I see no way to describe the [Drenthe] landscape as it ought to be described, since words fail me. But imagine the banks of the canal as miles and miles of Michels or Th. Rousseaus, for instance, Van Goyens or Ph. de Konincks. Flat planes or strips, of different colours, which become narrower and narrower as they approach the horizon, accentuated here and there by a turf hut or small farm or a couple of gaunt birches, poplars, oaks – everywhere piles of turf and barges sailing by with peat or flag from the marshes'. The modern world had not yet encroached upon the moors of isolated Drenthe. Though factories and trains do figure in Van Gogh's landscapes later in his career, in Drenthe he delighted in an environment 'where things haven't got any further than stagecoaches and canalboats, where *everything is much less spoiled than any place I've ever seen*'. Time and again he was surprised by 'all the variety in the seemingly monotonous countryside'. In the late

Vincent van Gogh
Heath at Nightfall
Watercolour, 41.5 × 53.7 cm - September 1883
Inv. D 386 M/1977 - F 1099

afternoon especially the light changed and the landscape became 'sublime', which explains why Vincent captured most of his views of Drenthe just prior to sunset. He worked not only in oil and watercolour but also in ink, 'with a view to the painting, because one can go into much greater detail with the pen than with the brush'.

Though this lovely Drenthe watercolour recalls work by members of the Hague School who excelled at the technique, Van Gogh drew most of his inspiration from French art during the months he spent in Drenthe: 'Think of Barbizon, that's a marvellous story. Those who started out there – not all of them were by any means what they seemed to be. The countryside formed them. All they knew is: "it's no good in the city, I've got to get out [...]. I'm going to renew myself in the country"'.

Vincent van Gogh
Farmhouses
Canvas, 35 × 55.5 cm - September 1883
Inv. S 53 V/1962 - F 17

Though desolate Drenthe was not particularly popular among artists, several of Van Gogh's confrères had preceded him to the outstretched moors of this northeastern Dutch province. His awareness of this precedent is evinced by his account of an excursion to picturesque Zweeloo, 'the village where [the German painter] Liebermann stayed for a long time and made studies for his picture of the last [Paris] Salon, with the washing women. Where Termeulen and Jules Bakhuyzen spent a lot of time'. Van Gogh's cousin Anton Mauve and his friend Anthon van Rappard had worked in Drenthe as well. Yet the painters he most often mentioned were those of the Barbizon School, especially Daubigny, Dupré and Michel. It was with their work in mind

that he explored the Drenthe countryside. Of the work Vincent produced during his three months in the province, between 11 September and 5 December 1883, little actually survives. We know of only five canvases, three of which are preserved by the Van Gogh Museum.

Farmhouses may be one of the first paintings Vincent sent Theo, in late September. The houses themselves, which barely protrude above the boggy moors, are characteristically constructed out of turf, moss and reed, and actually embedded in the ground. The artist's memory of a work by Dupré in the collection of the Hague painter H.W. Mesdag doubtless influenced the final result: '[a canvas] showing two cottages, their mossy roofs of a surprisingly deep

tone against a hazy, dusty evening sky'. The other illustrated canvas with a house of this kind – 'with a delicate green cornfield in the foreground, withered grasses behind the house and piles of peat' – was painted several weeks later.

Whereas his friend Van Rappard had painted a characteristic old woman from Drenthe, Van Gogh had difficulty finding models willing to sit for him. Indeed the illustrated oil sketch of two women digging peat constitutes the only figure piece he is known to have painted in the province. The women, who are little more than silhouettes, are reminiscent of Millet's *Gleaners*, while the evening sky recalls the French master's equally famous *Angelus*.

Vincent van Gogh
Farmhouse with Peat-stacks
Canvas, 37.5 × 55.5 cm - October/November 1883
Inv. S 130 V/1962 - F 22

Vincent van Gogh
Two Women in a Peat-field
Canvas, 27.5 × 36.5 cm - October 1883
Inv. S 129 V/1962 - F 19

On 31 December 1883 a certain notary in Nuenen by the name of Schutjes organised a lumber sale, and Van Gogh recorded the event.

The sign of the inn where the auction was held can be seen on the left. The notary is clearly visible on a small platform at the back of the crowd. In early 1884 Vincent wrote Theo about a drawing he had made, 'though only an impression, of a lumber sale'. The motif calls to mind the scene of people gathered in front of the State Lottery Office in The Hague, which Van Gogh drew in 1882. Rather than painting this watercolour on the spot, the artist probably did so in the studio, with the help of sketches.

Van Gogh was presumably familiar with a watercolour of a similar subject – a lumber sale in a forest – by his cousin Anton Mauve, now in the Museum Hendrik Willem Mesdag in The Hague.

Van Gogh in Nuenen and Antwerp

Ringed by outstretched moors, Nuenen lies several kilometres southeast of Eindhoven, in the heart of Brabant. In late 1883, a total of 2,560 people lived in the village. Half of the labour force were farm workers, the other half cottage weavers.

Though South Brabant was (and is) predominantly Roman Catholic, there was a small Protestant congregation in Nuenen. In March 1875 Reverend Theodorus van Gogh, the father of Vincent, was offered the rectorate of Nuenen. There was also a vacancy in the village of Etten-Leur, however, which he chose instead. But when, in late 1881, the Nuenen rectorate became available once again, Reverend van Gogh finally relented, and formally assumed his responsibilities on 12 August 1882.

On about 5 December 1883 Vincent van Gogh arrived in Nuenen. Since his relationship with his parents had been deteriorating, his arrival was not a particularly happy occasion. Vincent knew they dreaded having a maladjusted artist – like 'a big shaggy dog' – around the house.

'He'll come into the room with wet paws, and he's so shaggy. He'll get in everyone's way. *And he barks so loud*. In short, he's a filthy beast'. The first fourteen days were rather awkward, but a frank conversation cleared the air somewhat and on 20 December 1883 Reverend van Gogh wrote his son Theo that it had 'gradually got better, especially since we agreed to his staying with us so he could make some studies here. He hoped the mangle room could be furnished for him; we don't think that's really a suitable place to live, but we've had a decent heater put into it [...]. So we're facing this new test in good spirits essentially, and have decided not to do anything about his peculiar clothes and so forth. By now the people here have seen him and though it's still a pity that he doesn't act more obliging, there's no changing his eccentricity. He certainly works hard and finds more than enough material here for studies, several of which we find quite beautiful'.

Vincent van Gogh
The Garden of the Vicarage in Nuenen in Winter: 'Mélancholie'
Pencil and ink, 29 × 21 cm - December 1883
Inv. D 87 V/1962

Vincent van Gogh
Weaver in his Loom
Pencil and watercolour, 32 × 44 cm - 1884
Inv. D 85 V/1962 - F 1125

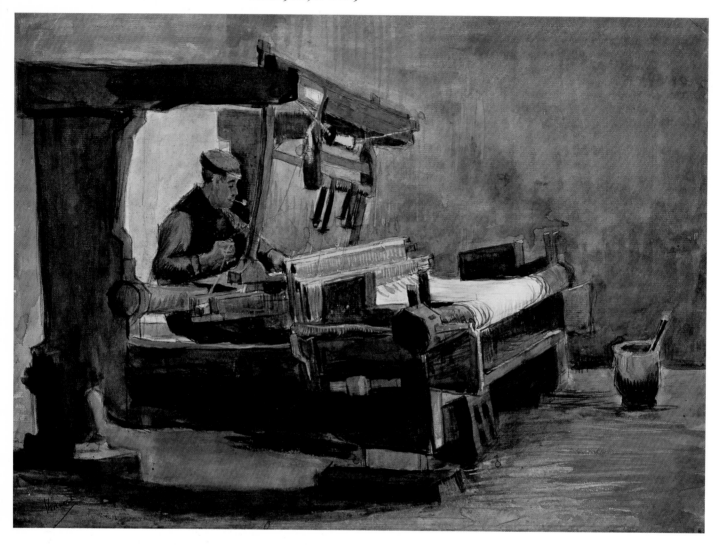

While living in The Hague, Van Gogh had read in Michelet's *Le Peuple* (1846) that the textile industry was responsible for creating 'a pathetic, misshapen kind of machine people, who were only capable of leading half a life'.
The artist himself described the weavers he witnessed in Nuenen as 'very pathetic little people', an impression the statistics confirm. As a rule the weavers lived at subsistence level and were decidedly poorer than the peasant population, who themselves could hardly be described as well off. In a letter written in September 1880 from the Borinage, Van Gogh already expressed compassion for the weavers, 'compared to other workers and artisans, a totally different sort of people'. He was moved by their 'dreamy, absent faces, like sleepwalkers'. They were 'the lowest of the low, so to speak, and the most despised'. In George Eliot's *Silas Marner* (1861), which Van Gogh read in 1876 and 1878, the weavers are described as pale runts who, compared to the robust country folk, looked like the last surviving members of an underprivileged race.
Between December 1883 and June 1884 Van Gogh busily depicted the weaving, yarn-spinning and reeling Brabanters, who comprised a quarter of Nuenen's labour force. In January 1884 he wrote: 'These people are difficult to draw, the rooms being so small that it's

impossible to get far enough away to sketch the loom'. Nonetheless he managed to record the machinery with surprising technical precision. 'I'm also painting a loom – made of old, greenish, browned oak – on which the year *1730* is carved. Near that loom, at a small window looking out on a green plot, is a baby's chair. The child sits in it for hours, watching the shuttle fly to a fro'. In the evening they went on working by the light of an oil lamp, thus creating 'very Rembrandtesque effects'. Van Gogh tenderly recalled the old-fashioned 'lamp, like the one in Millet's *La Veillée*, for instance', which a weaver had once given him.

Vincent van Gogh
Weaver in his Loom
Pencil and watercolour, 35 × 45 cm - 1884
Inv. D 371 V/1962 - F 1114

Vincent van Gogh
Man Winding Yarn
Watercolour, 46.7 × 34 cm - 1884
Inv. D 387 V/1977 - F 1140

Vincent van Gogh
Spinning Wheel
Oil on canvas, 34 × 44 cm - 1884
Inv. S 54 V/1963 - F 175

Van Gogh's father was the sole Protestant parson in a predominantly Roman Catholic community. Only four percent of the inhabitants of Nuenen was Protestant. The small church where the Reverend Van Gogh officiated, built in 1824, is still standing. Vincent made a painting of it for his mother in January 1884. Initially he placed a peasant with a spade over his shoulder in the foreground, only to overpaint the figure later with a group of believers leaving the church after a service.

Van Gogh executed the small picture of the parsonage not long before he left Nuenen, in October 1885. He had lived there himself between December 1883 and the following May, during which period he made several beautiful drawings of the garden.

The artist never mentioned the canvas with the parsonage in his letters, unlike the large illustrated landscape which he described as 'a rather large study of a road lined with poplars with yellow autumn leaves, the sun casting bright spots on the fallen leaves on the ground, which alternate with the long shadows of the trunks. At the end of the road [is seen] a small peasant house with blue sky above it, amid the autumn leaves'. In the same letter of late October 1884, Vincent reflected on 'impressionism', which Theo had written him about. In Paris, he realised, 'pictures are beginning to be painted in a very different tone than they were some years ago'. His own palette still differed radically from the chromatic ideal of the innovators in France. Indeed he predicted his own work would 'get a bit gloomier sooner than it would get lighter'.

Vincent van Gogh
The Vicarage at Nuenen
Canvas, 33 × 43 cm - 1885
Inv. S 140 V/1962 - F 182

Vincent van Gogh
Leaving the Church at Nuenen
Canvas, 41.5 × 32 cm - 1884
Inv. S 03 V/1962 - F 25

Vincent van Gogh
Avenue of Poplars in Autumn
Canvas on panel, 98.5 × 66 cm - 1884
Inv. S 141 M/1977 - F 122

In Nuenen, between painting landscapes and scenes from peasant life, Van Gogh created over a dozen still lifes. The genre was apparently compatible with teaching a number of amateur painters, which he did in Eindhoven in exchange for tubes of paint. As he wrote his brother in November 1884, 'I now have three people in Eindhoven who want to learn to paint. I'm teaching them how to make still lifes'. His pupils included a goldsmith turned antique dealer by the name of Hermans (for whose house he had designed a decoration), the tanner Anton Kerssemakers and the postal worker Willem van de Wakker. Some of Van de Wakker's recollections of Vincent's instruction survive. It seems they met through a paint dealer by the name of Baaiens, whom the artist patronised. While studying under Anton Mauve, Van Gogh's own first picture had been a still life. According to Van de Wakker, he impressed upon his pupils that 'Painting still lifes is the start of everything. If you can do a still life, you can also do a forest'.

Van Gogh's ideal of a still-life painter was the eighteenth-century Frenchman Jean-Siméon Chardin, whose predilection for humble, everyday objects he shared. Though Van de Wakker recalled that in Eindhoven, Van Gogh borrowed antiques from his pupil Hermans's collection for his still lifes, it was the simplest that he invariably chose: bottles, boxes, pots and stoneware tankards. Painting these modest objects was all Van Gogh needed to test the French colour theories he had been reading about. Indeed when discussing colour theory with his Dutch colleagues, he indicated the colours in French.

Vincent van Gogh
Still Life with Pottery, Bottles and a Box
Canvas, 31 × 41 cm - 1884
Inv. S 60 V/1962 - F 61 recto

Vincent van Gogh
Still Life with Three Beer Mugs
Canvas, 32 × 43 cm - 1885
Inv. S 96 V/1962 - F 49

Vincent van Gogh
Still Life with Pottery and Three Bottles
Canvas, 39 × 56 cm - 1885
Inv. S 138 V/1962 - F 53

Vincent van Gogh
Still Life with Honesty (sketch belonging to
letter 493 of 5 April 1885)

Vincent van Gogh
Vase with Honesty
Canvas, 42.5 × 31.5 cm - 1884
Inv. S 09 V/1962 - F 76

The still life with the 'honesty and withered leaves against blue', which Van Gogh mentions in a letter of about 1 April 1885, can probably be identified with the illustrated canvas. The artist's uncle, the dealer C.M. van Gogh, had criticised the work, prompting him to make another attempt. A mere four days later he sketched the second version in a letter to Theo dated 5 April. The contents of the letter suggest that his brother had taken the first version of the still life with him when he left Nuenen at the end of a previous visit. Vincent's sketch of the still life in his letter to Theo is one of the few of its kind that he made in watercolour. In effect it is an homage to his father, who had died unexpectedly on March 26th: 'the objects in the foreground are a tobacco pouch and a pipe that belonged to Pa'. The painting no longer exists as it was later painted over by the artist. In September 1885 he used the canvas to paint a still life with apples. The only remaining eulogy to Rev. van Gogh is the still life *Open Bible, Extinguished Candle and Novel*, painted in the autumn of 1885.

In the winter of 1884/85 Van Gogh painted no less than forty studies of Nuenen peasant heads. After the series published in the English magazine *The Graphic* he entitled them 'Heads of the People'. In October 1884 he had written his brother of wanting to paint about thirty, and by November he had already painted some fifty of them. The entire series he hoped to finish by January 1885. Vincent approached these studies as training for a career as a portraitist: 'There is more and more demand for portraits – and there are not so many who can do them. I want to try and learn how to paint a head with character'. Creating an exact likeness was not his primary goal; rather, he strove to capture whatever was characteristic, which is what he admired about the heads of Daumier.

His taste ran to models with something Millet-like about them: 'crude, flat faces with low foreheads and thick lips – not that sharpness, but full'. We know the artist had difficulty finding models – when, that is, he had money to pay them. In the winter this was a bit easier, since agriculture came to a halt. During this period Van Gogh worked with intense pleasure: 'those heads of local women with their white hats – it's difficult, but so incredibly beautiful. They're precisely *clair-obscur* – the white and part of the face in shadow are of such a fine tone'.

The picture of a woman painted in March 1885 is not only the most beautiful in Van Gogh's series of peasant studies, but also one of the few heads he deemed worthy of his signature. The following April he wrote his brother that he had made a pendant for it. Apparently he felt the series came close enough to his ideal – the 'Heads of the People' in *The Graphic* – to qualify as autonomous works. 'Indeed it's difficult to say where a study ends and a painting begins'. The model, Gordina de Groot, figures prominently in Van Gogh's *The Potato Eaters*. She was nearly thirty at the time.

Vincent van Gogh
Head of a Peasant Woman with White Cap
Canvas, 43 × 33.5 cm - March 1885
Inv. S 139 V/1962 - F 130

Vincent van Gogh
Head of a Peasant Woman with White Cap
Canvas, 42 × 34 cm - December 1884
Inv. S 72 V/1962 - F 156

Vincent van Gogh
Head of a Young Peasant with Pipe
Canvas, 38 × 30 cm - winter 1884/85
Inv. S 69 V/1962 - F 164

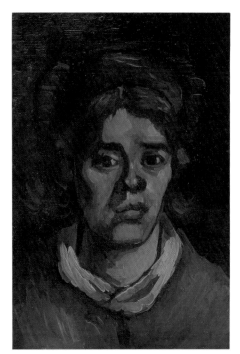

Vincent van Gogh
Head of a Peasant Woman
Canvas, 43.5 × 30 cm - March/April 1885
Inv. S 84 V/1962 - F 69

Vincent van Gogh
Head of a Peasant Woman with Red Bonnet
Canvas, 43 × 30 cm - April 1885
Inv. S 06 V/1962 - F 160

Vincent van Gogh
Head of a Peasant Woman
Canvas, 42 × 34 cm - April 1885
Inv. S 97 V/1962 - F 269 recto

Vincent van Gogh
Head of a Peasant Woman with White Cap
Canvas, 43.5 × 35.5 cm - May 1885
Inv. S 04 V/1962 - F 388 recto

The Potato Eaters is undoubtedly the most important work Van Gogh produced in Nuenen. With this canvas he realised his long-cherished dream of creating a figure piece in the peasant genre that measured up to his hero Millet. He may have become interested in the motif as early as 1882, when he saw a picture at the Hague branch of Goupil's showing a peasant family at table by Jozef Israëls. Treatments of similar motifs by such artists as Charles de Groux and Léon Lhermitte may have also inspired him. Only after drawing and painting numerous studies of peasant heads in Nuenen did Van Gogh feel up to the challenge, and in the course of 1885 the work began to take shape.

At first he could not decide whether the lighting should be natural or artificial, but finally settled on the latter. An oil study from February/March with four peasants round a table already approximates the definitive composition. On about 11 April 1885 Vincent wrote his brother that he had made a large oil sketch on canvas which in his estimation had 'some life to it'. That same month the Eindhoven lithographer Dimmen Gestel helped him make a litho of the composition, which constitutes an interesting intermediary stage in the evolution of the work. Van Gogh based the litho on the painted study now in the Rijksmuseum Kröller-Müller. He apparently intended to use the litho to solicit reactions to the projected painting from friends and colleagues, and even toyed with the idea of publishing it in the Parisian magazine *Le chat noir*. In the event his friend Anthon van Rappard's reaction was so critical that it effectively ended their relationship.

Ultimately – following 'a tremendous struggle' – Van Gogh painted the definitive picture from memory. The working method was inspired by Delacroix, the dark palette by Israëls and Millet. Théophile Gautier's evocative description of Millet's *Sower* – showing 'peasants painted with the earth they work' – is clearly echoed by the results. Vincent himself said he was trying to achieve the effect 'of a good dusty potato, unpeeled of course'. Even after his style had long since taken a very different direction under the influence of French Impressionism, he still considered *The Potato Eaters* '*après tout* the best [...] I've done'.

Vincent van Gogh
Four Peasants at Table
Canvas, 33 × 41 cm - February/March 1885
Inv. S 135 V/1962 - F 77

Vincent van Gogh
The Potato Eaters
Litho, 36.5 × 32 cm - April 1885
Inv. P 16 V/1962 - F 1661

Vincent van Gogh
The Potato Eaters
Canvas, 82 × 114 cm - April 1885
Inv. S 05 V/1962 - F 82

'What I've tried to do is convey the idea that those people, eating their potatoes by lamplight, have dug the earth with the very hands they put into their bowls. Thus it's about *manual labour*, and about the fact that they've *earned* their food so honestly. I wanted it to make people think about an entirely different way of life than that of us civilised people. So I'm not at all concerned whether everyone likes it straight away or not. All winter long I've had the threads of this tissue in my hands, and have searched for the ultimate pattern; and if it's a tissue that appears rough or coarse, at least the threads have been chosen carefully and in accordance with certain rules. And it might prove to be a *true peasant picture. I know that's what it is.* But if someone prefers a sentimental view of peasants, they're welcome to it. As for myself, I'm convinced you get better results by painting them in their roughness than by bringing conventional charm into it'. (Vincent to Theo, ca. 20 April 1885)

In May 1885 Van Gogh finished two important pictures which, together with *The Potato Eaters*, amount to a triptych of rural life. Around the eleventh of the month he wrote his brother about 'a large study of a cottage at dusk' he was working on, and a painting of the old church tower that was about to be pulled down – indeed the spire was 'already gone'. In early June Vincent sent *The Cottage* to Theo in Paris, and the *Country Churchyard with Old Church Tower* shortly thereafter. To underscore the autonomy of both works, he assigned formal French titles to them: *La chaumière* and *Cimetière de Paysans*. Van Gogh became interested in cottages with thatched roofs while living in Drenthe. His pictures of them recall a canvas by the Barbizon painter Jules Dupré 'with two cottages, their thatched roofs of a surprisingly deep tone against a hazy, dusty evening sky'. He thought of these cottages as 'human nests'; more specifically, they reminded him of a wren's nest, like that he had just found. Vincent's fascination with the Nuenen churchyard can be traced back to September 1882, while he was still living in The Hague. 'I can't stop thinking about that churchyard with those old crosses. I really hope I'll get around to doing it in due time'. At that point he was planning to paint a peasant funeral in the snow, and before leaving Drenthe had already sketched a simple churchyard he stumbled upon in the midst of the moors. In early June 1885 Van Gogh explained the significance of the *Country Church-yard with Old Church Tower* to his brother. 'I wanted to express how the ruins show that *for centuries* peasants

Vincent van Gogh
Country Churchyard with Old Church Tower
Canvas, 63 × 79 cm - May 1885
Inv. S 02 V/1962 - F 84

have been laid to rest there in the very fields they worked – I wanted to show how utterly simple death and burial are, as nice as the falling of the autumn leaves – just some earth dug up, a wooden cross. The surrounding fields – they make a final line against the horizon above the wall where the grass of the graveyard ends, like a horizon at sea. That ruin tells me how a creed and a religion have mouldered away, even though they were well established – how nevertheless the life and death of the peasants is always the same:

constantly sprouting and withering like the grass and the flowers growing there in the churchyard. "Les religions passent, Dieu demeure," as Victor Hugo put it, whom they've just buried'. Van Gogh's critical attitude toward religion is doubtless related to his difficult relationship with his father, who had died recently and been buried in this very churchyard.

In St-Rémy in April 1890 Van Gogh considered making new versions of both pictures. Though he never did so, several months later he sent his sister a

description of the picture he was painting of the Auvers village church – which shows just how much he still had his Nuenen work in mind. 'Again the [theme] is almost identical to the studies of the old tower and the churchyard I made in Nuenen', he wrote. 'Only now the colour is probably more expressive, fuller'.

Vincent van Gogh
Basket with Potatoes
Canvas, 44.5 × 60 cm - September 1885
Inv. S 153 V/1962 - F 100

These still lifes can be dated on the basis of a letter Vincent wrote Theo in late September 1885, explaining the four canvases he had just sent. 'What I have for you are some still lifes – a basket of potatoes, fruit, a copper kettle, etc. – which are really about modelling with various colours'. Félix Bracquemond's book *Du dessin et de la couleur* had got him interested in using colour this way. After sending the works to Theo in Paris, Vincent elaborated on how he had employed colour in the four works. The potato still lifes were conceived as variations on the theme of brownish grey. In a still life with apples, he contrasted not only the complementary colours green and red, but also the fore- and backgrounds. 'I gave the one a natural colour by breaking blue with orange, and the other the same natural colour, except that I altered it by adding some yellow'. Many will find these still lifes unattractive, and indeed it is impossible to understand them without knowing something about the artist's colour experiments. When the painter Achille Cesbron dared to exhibit a still life with potatoes at the Paris Salon in 1888 he was promptly attacked by the critic Henry Houssaye: 'Mr Cesbron [...] offers us adorable potatoes in their jackets. O sancta simplicitas!' Van Gogh had no illusions about the commercial value of potato still lifes; they were strictly studies as far as he was concerned. Self-effacing as always, he concluded the previously quoted letter to his brother with a request: 'And if you find some book or other about colour, send it to me, would you? There's so much more I have to learn, and I try to learn more every day'.

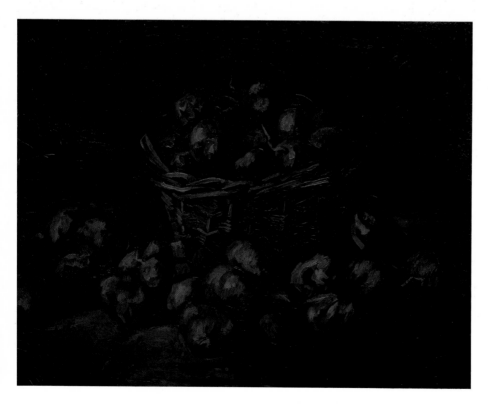

Vincent van Gogh
Basket with Potatoes
Canvas, 50.5 × 66 cm - September 1885
Inv. S 152 V/1962 - F 116

Vincent van Gogh
Basket with Potatoes
Canvas, 33 × 43.5 cm - September 1885
Inv. S 150 V/1962 - F 101

Vincent van Gogh
Still Life with Vegetables and Fruit
Canvas, 32.5 × 43 cm - September 1884
Inv. S 70 V/1962 - F 103

Vincent van Gogh
Still Life with Copper Kettle, Jug and Potatoes
Canvas, 65.5 × 80.5 cm - September 1885
Inv. S 52 V/1962 - F 51

Living in Nuenen Van Gogh developed a passion for collecting bird's nests, a passion he shared with his fellow painter Anthon van Rappard. Indeed he sent his friend a basket of them in September 1885. 'I too have some in my studio, quite a collection in fact, so I'm sending you some duplicates. They're of thrush, blackbird, golden oriole, wren and finch'. For Van Gogh, skilful nest builders 'such as wrens or golden orioles can surely be considered artists. At the same time [their nests] make beautiful still lifes'.

In early October Vincent wrote his brother that he had painted four still lifes, inspired by his collection of bird's nests. 'I think the colours of the moss, dry leaves and grasses, clay, etc. might appeal to people who know a good deal about nature. [...] Toward winter, if I

Vincent van Gogh
Two Bird's Nests
Canvas, 31.5 × 42.5 cm - September/October 1885. Inv. S 71 V/1962 - F 109 recto

have more time, I'll make some drawings of this sort of thing. *La nichée et les nids*, that's what I like – especially those *human* nests, those cottages on

the heath and their inhabitants'.

The nests, too, were colour studies first of all. Some of them are intentionally cast against a black background so as to indicate 'that the objects appear not in their natural surroundings, but against a conventional *fond*'. Though it was during that very period that he admired the coloured backgrounds of some still lifes in the Rijksmuseum, he decided against them in the end. 'A *living* nest in nature is something else altogether. One hardly sees the nest itself, one sees the birds. But since I want to paint nests *from my own nest collection*, I can't make it clear enough that the background is very different from the natural surroundings. I simply made the background black'.

Vincent van Gogh
Five Bird's Nests
Canvas, 39.5 × 46 cm - September/October 1885 Inv. S 01 V/1962 - F 111

During the second week of October 1885 Van Gogh spent three days in Amsterdam so he could visit the recently opened Rijksmuseum and the Fodor Collection. He took the opportunity to study seventeenth-century masters as well as the work of such contemporary artists as Jozef Israëls. Despite the brevity of his Amsterdam sojourn, he still found time to paint. 'The two small panels I painted in Amsterdam were done in great haste, one even in the waitingroom of the station [...], the other in the morning, before I went to the museum at about ten o'clock'.

This view of several tugs moored behind Amsterdam's railway station was probably the second of these 'small panels'. Vincent was so pleased with his 'little tiles, on which I just threw something down with a few strokes', that he sent them on to Theo, even though they were slightly damaged: 'they got wet en route, then the panels warped while drying, dust got into them, and so forth'.

He wanted to show his brother 'that if I want to spend an hour somewhere tossing off an impression I can just about do so, the same way others analyse their impressions and arrive at an understanding of what they see. That's something other than feeling, that's experiencing impressions – there may be a big difference between experiencing impressions and analysing them, that is *taking them apart and putting them back together again*. It's quite pleasant to throw

something down on the run'.

Van Gogh visited Amsterdam together with Anton Kerssemakers from Eindhoven, to whom he was giving painting lessons at that time. The watercolour of a rainy scene, which he inscribed 'Un dimanche à Eindhoven', is the same sort of rapid, evocative impression as that Vincent painted in Amsterdam.

Vincent van Gogh
Street in Eindhoven in the Rain
Watercolour, 20.9 × 29.5 cm - November 1885
Inv. D 47 V/1969 - F 1348

Vincent van Gogh
The Ruijterkade in Amsterdam with Tugboats
Panel, 20.5 × 27 cm - October 1885
Inv. S 85 V/1962 - F 211

Vincent van Gogh
Still Life with Open Bible, Extinguished Candle and Novel
Canvas, 65 × 78 cm - October 1885
Inv. S 08 V/1962 - F 117

Studying the masters of Holland's Golden Age in the Rijksmuseum reassured Van Gogh that his illustrious precursors would approve of his tonal manner. As he wrote his brother, who had advised him against using black, in October 1885, 'Rembrandt and Hals didn't use black? Or Velàzquez? Not only one, but twenty-seven blacks, I can assure you'. With that Theo qualified his position, citing the black in Manet's picture of a dead toreador (now in Washington's National Gallery of Art). To end the discussion Vincent painted the *Still Life with Bible, Extinguished Candle and Novel*. 'In reply to your description of the Manet study, I'm sending you a still life with an open (and therefore off-white) leatherbound Bible against a black background. The foreground is yellowish brown with a touch of lemon yellow. I painted it *all at once*, in one day'. Two of the three objects in this canvas – the open Bible and the extinguished candle – link it to the time-honoured tradition of the vanitas still life. The text can be identified as Isaiah 53, which proclaims the coming of the servant of the Lord, who shall be despised and rejected of men.

Besides the painterly dialogue with Manet, the still life also has a third dimension.

The Bible can be seen as an allusion to Vincent's father, Rev. Theodorus van Gogh, who died that year. The muted tones of the book, signifying his father's strict piety, contrast with the 'touch of lemon yellow' on the cover of the novel, *La joie de vivre* by the French Naturalist Emile Zola.

There has been a great deal of speculation about the meaning of the worn-out shoes, a theme Van Gogh returned to repeatedly over the years. Even such eminent thinkers as Heidegger and Derrida have tried their hand at them.

The artist's original intent is still uncertain, as is the date. While the canvas is usually assigned to the artist's Parisian period, some would argue it has more in common with his Nuenen work. In January 1894, in an article entitled 'Nature mortes', Paul Gauguin described just such a still life with shoes, which he associated with the artist's departure from Nuenen: 'In my small yellow room, a still life, this time violet. – Two enormous shoes, worn out, misshapen. Vincent's shoes. The pair he put on one morning when they were still new in order to hike from Holland to Belgium'.

Vincent van Gogh
A Pair of Shoes
Canvas, 37.5 × 45 cm - 1885/86
Inv. S 11 V/1962 - F 255

No sooner had Van Gogh arrived in Antwerp on 24 November 1885 than he set out to explore the city and its museums, paying particular attention to the work of Rubens. Here too, however, he found his greatest inspiration on the street: ordinary people who lived and worked in the Scheldt city. 'I see the people on the street – good, but I often find the maidservants so much more interesting and beautiful than the ladies – the labourers more interesting than the gentlemen. And in those ordinary young people I find a strength and vitality one would have to paint with a firm touch, a simple technique, in order to capture their singular character'. And before long he decided it was 'true on the whole what they say about Antwerp, the women are indeed beautiful'. In early December 1885 Van Gogh painted the heads of a young woman and an old man 'as portrait trials'. He was very taken with the 'splendid old man' he had found as a model, whose features reminded him of the writer Victor Hugo. The woman's countenance he rendered in light tones, 'white tinted with carmine, vermillion, yellow and a light background of greyish yellow, from which the face is only distinguished by the black hair. Lilac tones in the clothes'. Van Gogh hoped his female heads would sell, but when they failed to do so, he began painting views of the city as tourist souvenirs. 'Yet I prefer painting people's eyes to cathedrals, for however solemn and imposing it may be, there's something in their eyes the cathedral lacks, namely the human soul'.

The curious little canvas with a skeleton smoking is thought to be a joke Van Gogh made while studying at the Antwerp academy.

Vincent van Gogh
Head of a Woman with her Hair Loose
Canvas, 35 × 24 cm - December 1885
Inv. S 59 V/1962 - F 206

_____

_____

Vincent van Gogh
Skull with Burning Cigarette
Canvas, 32 × 24.5 cm - winter 1885/1886
Inv. S 83 V/1962 - F 212

_____

Vincent van Gogh
Head of an Old Man
Canvas, 44.5 × 33.5 cm
- December 1885
Inv. S 61 V/1962 -
F 205

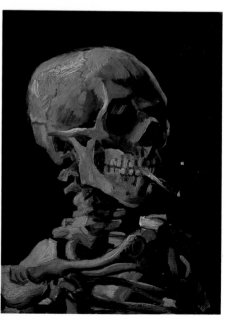

The intimate view of houses in the snow is one of the first oil studies Vincent made in Antwerp.

As he would later do in Paris he painted it from the window of his flat, located above a paint dealer on Rue des Images.

Vincent van Gogh
Backs of Houses in
Antwerp in the Snow
Canvas, 44 × 33.5 cm -
December 1885
Inv. S 142 V/1962

Vincent van Gogh
Dancing Women
Black and coloured chalk on vellum paper
9.2 × 16.4 cm - December 1885
Inv. D 27 V/1962 - F 1350b

The Van Gogh Museum preserves practically everything Van Gogh is known to have produced during the three months he spent in Antwerp. A number of the drawings apparently derive from sketchbooks. This is true of the three dance hall scenes, for instance, which are all of virtually the same size; only a few drawings from the sketchbook they belonged to are still known. In a letter to Theo of about 6-7 December 1885, Vincent described a visit to a hall like that in the illustrated sheet: 'Yesterday I was in the café-concert Scala, which is something like the Folies Bergères. I found it very dull and of course insipid, but the audience amused me. There were splendid women's heads, really extraordinarily beautiful, among the good burghers in the seats at the back [...]'.

In his search for models in the Flemish city Van Gogh was repeatedly struck by extremes. One moment he noticed a group of brawny sailors eating mussels, the next 'a Chinese girl, mysterious and quiet as a mouse, small, like a bedbug [...]. Now one sees a girl who is splendidly healthy and at least seems to be very loyal and naïvely gay, then again a face so sly and false that it frightens one, as a hyena would. Not to mention the faces scarred by smallpox, the colour of boiled shrimp, with pale grey eyes, without eyebrows, and thin, sleek hair the colour of real pig bristles or a bit yellower – Swedish or Danish types'.

Vincent van Gogh
Two Women in a Loge
Black and coloured chalk on vellum paper
9.5 × 16.5 cm - December 1885
Inv. D 25 V/1962 - F 1350v

Vincent van Gogh
Dance Hall
Black and coloured chalk on vellum paper
9.2 × 16.3 cm - December 1885
Inv. D 26 V/1962 - F 1350a

Vincent van Gogh
Portrait of a Woman
Black and coloured chalk on vellum paper
50.7 × 39.4 cm - winter 1885/86
Inv. D 58 V/1962 - F 1357

John Peter Russell
Darlinghurst 1858-1931 Sydney
Portrait of Vincent van Gogh
Canvas, 60 × 45 cm - 1886. Inv. S 273 V/1962

Paris in the 1880s

In the nineteenth century, Paris was indisputably the artistic capital of Europe. The 1880s in particular were distinguished by a compulsion to innovate that occasionally bordered on anarchy. Sooner or later every French painter with any ambition went to Paris, as indeed did many promising young artists from the rest of Europe and the United States.

Any artist who wished to succeed had to ensure that he or she stood out. In his *La Capitale de l'art* (1886) the authoritative critic Albert Wolff observed that 'In our day the painter is no longer a plodding artisan who shuts himself up and lives in a dream world behind locked doors. Rather he catapults himself headlong into the bustling life of the world and participates avidly in mondaine Parisian society; he has arrived if and when his studio becomes a salon where the elite convene'. The 1880s were a heyday for salon painters on the one hand, while on the other the leading Impressionists also managed to get a foot on the ground. Meanwhile another generation of artists had come forward, immortalised in the annals of art history as the Post-impressionists. It

was with this last group that, shortly after arriving in Paris in 1886, Vincent van Gogh cast his lot. When the obstreperous avant-garde encountered difficulty gaining admission to the Salon, the painters banded together and organised their own group shows. Between 1874 and 1886, the Impressionists staged eight controversial exhibitions. Artists of the next generation, such as Paul Gauguin, Georges Seurat and Paul Signac, were the most prominent at the Salons des Artistes Indépendants. The Parisian art market had long been lively. The most prominent firm was Goupil (the later Boussod, Valadon &

Cie), which operated internationally and dealt primarily in artists who were a bit more established. Paris also had a number of small but enterprising dealers such as Alphonse Portier, Julien-François Tanguy and Georges Thomas who were not afraid to represent young, relatively obscure artists. Partly under the influence of his brother Vincent, Theo van Gogh grew increasingly sympathetic to younger artists, even though he was employed by Goupil's. By degrees the Montmartre branch of Goupil's which Theo managed became a meeting place of the Parisian avant-garde.

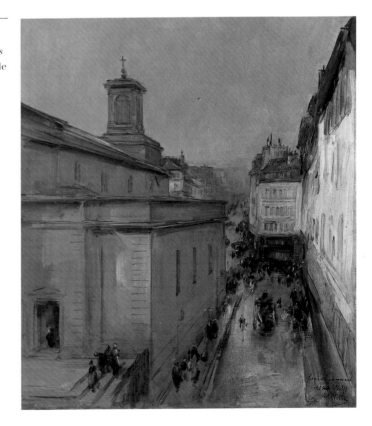

*Antoine Vollon
Lyons 1833-1900 Paris*
View of Notre Dame de Lorette and Rue Fléchier in Paris, dedicated to Albert Wolff
*Panel, 73.5 × 60 cm
Inv. S 99 B/1991,
on loan from the
Rijksmuseum*

Felician Freiherr von Myrbach-Rheinfeld
Galicia 1853-1940 Klagenfurt
Interior of a Print Shop
Canvas, 64.5 × 80.9 cm - 1884
Inv. S 432 M/1992

Countless foreign artists were drawn irresistably to Paris, the uncontested capital of the visual arts in the nineteenth century. The Austrian nobleman Von Myrbach settled there in 1883. Having initially aspired to a military career, he studied painting and even taught a bit of drawing at the same academy where his classmates studied warfare.

Upon arriving in Paris in 1883 he decided to finish his training under Carolus Duran, and that same year made his debut at the Salon with *Au boulevard St-Michel*. He exhibited this interior of a printing establishment under the title *Chez l'imprimeur en taille-douce* at the following Salon. The splendid light, the sober tones of brown, blue and grey, and the rhythmical arrangement of the levers of the six printing presses are especially noteworthy.

Von Myrbach illustrated the catalogue of the Salon with lithographs after his submissions. So well were these received that, somewhat to his own surprise, the art world came to think of him as an illustrator. It was in that capacity that he worked for, among others, *Paris Illustré* (published by Boussod, Valadon & Cie), illustrating the work of such writers as About, Coppée, Chamisso, Hugo and Mérimée. For Alphonse Daudet he illustrated *Tartarin de Tarascon* and *Tartarin sur les Alpes*, and *Madame Chrysanthème* for Pierre Loti – books dear to none other than Vincent van Gogh.

In 1897 Von Myrbach returned to Vienna, where he quickly became a prominent ally of the avant-garde. As director of the Kunstgewerbe Schule (between 1899 and 1905) and friend of Gustav Klimt, he played an influential role in the movement of the Vienna Secession.

The Norwegian artist Hans Olaf Heyerdahl was born in Sweden. Stylistically, his portraits and landscapes – the two genres in which he specialised – lie somewhere between Realism and Impressionism. Heyerdahl studied under Bonnat in Paris, and won a medal at the Exposition Internationale as early as 1878. Theo van Gogh was so impressed by the Scandinavian that in April 1881 he advised his brother Vincent to take lessons from him and, before long, started dealing in his work. As well as the two illustrated pictures, the brothers' collection comprised drawings of female figures; one of the sheets is a study for Heyerdahl's canvas *L'Enfant mourant*, which the French State purchased in 1882. During the early 1880s, Heyerdahl is mentioned repeatedly in the letters exchanged by Theo and Vincent, always in favourable terms. We read that Theo showed his brother's drawing *Sorrow* to Heyerdahl in June 1882, for instance, and that Vincent sent the Scandinavian a copy of his litho with the same theme the following November. In March 1884, when he complained that Theo was not doing enough to sell his work, Vincent adduced Heyerdahl's high estimation of him as a reason why his brother should do more. Finally, in a letter to their sister of 13 October 1885, Theo placed his brother on a par with the Scandinavian painter: 'As regards success, things may turn out for him [i.e. Vincent] as they have for Heyerdahl: appreciated by a few, but misunderstood by the general public. Yet he will win the respect of anyone who is really concerned whether an artist has something of value to offer or simply fool's gold [...]'.

Charles Antoine
Portrait of a Young Woman
Dedicated to Vincent van Gogh
Panel, 35 × 21 cm - 1886
Inv. S 203 V/1962

Vittorio Matteo Corcos
Livorno 1859-1933 Florence
Portrait of a Young Woman
Dedicated to Theo van Gogh
Canvas, 44 × 30 cm - 1884
Inv. S 216 V/1962

The small panel with a girl in rural dress, dedicated to 'mon ami Vincent', attests to Van Gogh's friendship with the painter Charles Antoine – otherwise known as Antonio Cristobal – during his first year in Paris. The two men met in Cormon's studio. A year after Van Gogh's death, in May 1891, Antoine published an article about his comrade in *La Butte*.

The Italian Vittorio Corcos, who dedicated his small portrait of a young woman to Theo van Gogh, was active in Paris between 1880 and 1886. Like his compatriot Federico Zandomeneghi, in whose work Theo also dealt, Corcos specialised in elegant women. His *Contemplation*, which dates from the late 1880s, shows a fashionable young woman in mourning, kneeling in a chapel. The older woman behind her, absorbed in devotional reading, is probably her chaperone. Though the young woman holds an open prayerbook, she fixes the viewer with a gaze not entirely consistent with either her sober costume or her gloomy surroundings.

Vittorio Matteo Corcos
Contemplation
Canvas, 86.5 × 79.2 cm
Inv. S 294 M/1974

Jacob van Looy studied at the Rijksacademie in Amsterdam, where he won the Prix de Rome in 1883. On the first leg of a journey to Italy and Spain in 1886 he also visited Paris. Though to our knowledge he did not meet Van Gogh, he did manage to absorb enough of what was happening in the studios to attune this street scene perfectly to the art younger artists were producing in the French capital. Seurat and Bernard were also painting women in the light of gas lanterns at that time.

Lévy, a pupil of Abel de Pujol and
François Picot, won the Grand Prix de
Rome in 1854, and became famous as a
history painter after the French State
purchased his *Mort d'Orphée* in 1866,
which now hangs in the Musée d'Orsay.
The following year he received the
Légion d'honneur.
The critic José Maria de Heredia
considered Lévy one of the most
original artists working in pastel at the
time. Around 1875 Lévy began painting
girls in kimonos, the theme that would
become his trademark. In February
1885 Van Gogh wrote his brother that
he had been particularly struck by an
illustration of 'a figure of a girl by Emile
Lévy, Japonaise' in a publication about
the Salon of 1884. Lévy's large pastel
Pensive Girl does indeed have a certain
Japanese air. The work may be
identical with a pastel portrait of
'Mademoiselle H.C.', displayed at the
Salon of 1888. In his review of that
exhibition, the critic Henry Houssaye
praised 'the lovely style, the lively
grace, the fluency of the chalk and the
extraordinary relief'.

Emile Lévy
Paris 1826-1890 Paris
Pensive Girl
Pastel, 102.5 × 63.5 cm - 1888
Inv. D 1009 M/1991

Georges Jeannin
Paris 1841-1925 Lagny-sur-Marne
Vase with Flowers
Panel, 37 × 20 cm
Inv. S 234 V/1962

Georges Jeannin
Vase with Flowers
Canvas, 70 × 46 cm
Inv. S 235 V/1962

When Vincent van Gogh described to his brother the profusion of flowers in Arles, it was not so much of Fantin-Latour that he was thinking as of Manet and two other artists who are now less well known, namely Ernest Quost and Georges Jeannin. Jeannin specialised in 'splendid bouquets of peonies' to quote Vincent, who hoped to match him one day with his sunflowers. So highly did the Dutch artist esteem Jeannin as a colourist that he placed him on a par with Daubigny. Shortly before his death, in late June 1890, Van Gogh expressed a desire to see Jeannin again in Paris. His curiosity had apparently been piqued by a remark his brother made in a letter of 23 June, that the flowers Jeannin exhibited at the last Salon 'explode off the canvas'.

Adolphe Monticelli is also regularly mentioned in Vincent's letters from Arles. He and Theo had collected a number of the French painter's works. In August 1888, Vincent alluded to the illustrated panel in describing to his brother the countryside, which 'shimmers like the bouquet by Monticelli you have'. Vincent was very proud of this particular still life, which he considered 'more artistic and more beautiful than a bouquet by Diaz'.

Adolphe Monticelli
Marseilles 1824-1886 Marseilles
Arabs and a Horseman
Canvas, 38 × 46 cm - 1871
Inv. S 250 V/1962

'[...] a great man – a little disturbed, or
rather very much so – dreaming of sun
and love and joy, but always plagued by
poverty, with a highly refined feeling for
colour, a man of rare class who upheld
the best old traditions. He died rather
sadly in Marseilles, probably after going
through a real Gethsemane. As for myself,
I'm certain that I'm going on with his
work here, just as if I were his son or
brother [...]'
'Monticelli is a painter who did the south
all in yellow, all in orange, all in sulphur.
Most painters, because they aren't
colourists in the true sense of the word,
don't see those colours there, and they
call a painter mad if he sees with eyes
other than theirs'.
*(Van Gogh to his sister Wil, Arles,
August 1888)*

Adolphe Monticelli
Moslims in Front of a Mosque
Panel, 44.5 × 40 cm
Inv. S 339 V/1966

Adolphe Monticelli
Festival in Venice
Canvas, 47.5 × 98.5 cm
Inv. S 341 V/1966

Adolphe Monticelli
Woman with a Parasol
Panel, 50 × 25 cm - ca. 1879
Inv. S 253 V/1962

Artistically Van Gogh regarded Monticelli as a direct descendant of Delacroix. The Dutchman's famous letter of early 1890 to the critic Albert Aurier, in which he designated the painters Narcisse Diaz de la Peña and Félix Ziem as links between Monticelli and Delacroix, shows how well he was informed about Monticelli's career. Ever since 1864 Joseph Delarbeyrette had been Monticelli's principal dealer in Paris, and it was at his gallery that Van Gogh encountered the Frenchman's art for the first time. For his part, Theo van Gogh had already sold three works by Monticelli for Boussod & Valadon before his brother moved to Paris, in 1885. Vincent's enthusiasm for the painter was such that he and Theo hatched a plan to compete with Delarbeyrette. Between 1887 and 1890 Theo sold almost twenty works by the master from Marseilles. The brothers retained six Monticellis for their own collection.

While living in Arles Vincent was always on the lookout for new business. On 24 September 1888 he wrote his brother about figures by Monticelli 'such as the yellow woman, such as the woman with the parasol, the small one you have [...], those are full figures which, as regards the draughtsmanship, you can't help but admire. Monticelli knows how to make a full, superb drawing like Daumier and Delacroix. At the prices Monticellis are going for nowadays you'd certainly do well to buy them. The day will come when his beautiful *drawn* figures will be appreciated as very great art indeed'. On Vincent's initiative, Boussod & Valadon published a lavishly illustrated album about Monticelli in 1890. The text was written by the poet Paul Guigou – not to be confused with the homonymous painter – and the twenty lithographs were made by Auguste Lauzet. Three of the works illustrated in the album belonged to the Van Gogh brothers' collection.

As well as a still-life painter of note, Monticelli was an innovative landscapist. In St-Rémy, Van Gogh was often reminded of landscapes by the Frenchman he had seen in Paris. As he wrote his brother in October 1889, 'Do you remember that beautiful landscape by Monticelli that we saw with Delarbeyrette, showing a tree on the rocks at sunset? There are a lot of those effects at the moment'. The brothers themselves owned none of Monticelli's landscapes, however; the illustrated panel was in a Dutch private collection before entering the Van Gogh Museum in the 1960s.

As a landscapist, Monticelli was influenced by Corot, Diaz and his teacher Félix Ziem, who accompanied him on painting expeditions to the woods around Fontainebleau. Many of his landscapes are set in Provence, where he often worked side by side with the painter Paul Guigou.
As early as 1860, Corot prompted the Palais des Beaux-Arts in Lille to purchase one of Monticelli's landscapes. The poet Paul Verlaine was another early collector of his work.

Adolphe Monticelli
Marseilles 1824-1886 Marseilles
Landscape
Panel, 40 × 60 cm
Inv. S 340 V/1966

Paul Guigou
Villars 1834-1871 Paris
Landscape near St-Paul-la-Durance
Panel, 21.9 × 46 cm - 1869
Inv. S 422 M/1991

As a fellow habitué of the renowned Café Guerbois, Guigou rubbed elbows with the Impressionists in the late 1860s. Following a rather unsettled period as a result of the Franco-Prussian War, he died unexpectedly in 1871 and his work was quickly forgotten. His untimely death prevented him from witnessing the radical innovations made by the Impressionists. Yet, inspired by the intense light of southern France, where he found his themes in the rough landscape, Guigou had already lightened his palette of his own accord.

Forbidden by his family to pursue a career in art, Guigou studied to become a notary but spent more time on his painting than he did on the law. His drawing instructor advised him to work *en plein air*. During his notarial apprenticeship in Marseilles he met both Monticelli and the noted Provençal poet Frédéric Mistral, who would later declare Guigou 'the greatest painter of Provence'. Under Monticelli's influence, he developed a freer, sketch-like manner. In 1861 Guigou's parents relented and he was finally allowed to devote himself entirely to art. Together with Monticelli he left for Paris, where he made his debut at the following Salon. The focus of his work remained his native Provence, to which he returned each summer. From 1864 he stayed near the village of St-Paul on the river Durance, pictured here in our panel.

One of Guigou's teachers was Emile Loubon (1809-1863). In an effort to effect a cultural renascence in Provence, Loubon did much to convince artists that the region was worth painting. His untimely death in 1863 prevented him from seeing his dream realised in the art of Guigou and Monticelli, and then crowned in that of Cézanne and Van Gogh.

Victor Vignon
Villers-Cotterêts 1847-1909 Meulan
Woman in a Vineyard
Canvas, 27 × 40 cm
Inv. S 277 V/1962

Victor Vignon
View of a Small Town
Canvas, 27 × 41 cm
Inv. S 278 V/1962

Victor Vignon carved out a place for himself among the minor masters of Impressionism. A friend of Van Gogh's, he owned no less than three of the Dutch artist's works. Despite his affiliation with the Impressionists, with whom he regularly exhibited, Vignon managed to navigate around the storms

that beset painting in the 1880s. In 1878 he was admitted to the Salon, but subsequently threw his lot in with the Impressionists. Participating in their last four exhibitions, between 1880 and 1886, he achieved a modicum of success, though Edouard Manet's brother Eugène accused him of reverting to his 'imitations of Corot'. Vignon was the son of the sculptress and writer Claude Vignon, pseudonym of Noémie Cadiot (1832-1888). Though he studied painting under Corot and was also influenced by Cals, he regarded the Old Masters in the Louvre as his true models. As a landscape painter he found his themes near Chatou, Bougival (where Daubigny also worked), Pontoise and Auvers-sur-Oise (where he associated with Cézanne, Guillaumin and Pissarro). In Auvers, Dr Gachet and the *pâtissier poète* Eugène Murer were among his contacts. Our knowledge of Vignon's relationship with the brothers Van Gogh is super-ficial at best. If the concern Vincent occasionally voiced about the artist's living conditions are any indication, they must have been close friends. In July 1888, Vignon was – along with Gauguin and Bernard – one of three artists Vincent hoped would join him in Arles. Following his crisis, moreover, while on the lookout for an alternative to the asylum of St-Rémy, Vincent suggested to Theo that he lodge with Vignon: 'It'd be better to use the money to feed painters than to give it to the worthy nuns'.

On 10 March 1888 Vincent van Gogh wrote his brother from Arles, 'I've gotten to know a Danish artist who talks about Heyerdahl and other people from the north, De Kroyer and so forth. What he makes is dull but very meticulous, and he is still young. He saw the Impressionist exhibitions in Rue Lafitte. He will probably come to Paris for the Salon and would like to come to Holland to see the museums'. The young artist was Christian Mourier-Petersen, a 'rank beginner' in Van Gogh's eyes.

He had come to the south of France to recover from a mental illness caused by his problems with medical school, according to Vincent. Mourier-Petersen regularly accompanied him on painterly excursions. The two artists would spend the evenings talking about the novels of Zola, Goncourt and Maupassant – and, of course, the Impressionists, 'all of whom he knew by name or from their pictures'.

During that period the Danish artist portrayed a girl from Arles, who may have also sat for Van Gogh's *Mousmé* later on. Vincent took a benign view of his young confrère: 'an intelligent fellow, [...] very trustworthy and well-mannered, but' – he wrote Theo on 9 April 1888 – 'his painting is still very poor'. By the time Mourier-Petersen left Paris in mid-May, however, his work already had more colour. Van Gogh provided introductions to the painters Russell and Koning, and gave him two small pictures to present to Countess de la Boissière in Asnières. For much of the time he spent in Paris the Dane lodged with Theo van Gogh.

Later that year Mourier-Petersen did indeed visit the Netherlands, and wrote Van Gogh what he had seen on 25 January 1889. In both the Mauritshuis and the Rijksmuseum he had painted copies after Rembrandt, besides acquainting himself with the work of the Dutch painters Mauve, Israëls and Breitner; in his opinion these nineteenth-century masters 'do not make enough effort to look with their eyes'. The contemporary Scandinavian painters received equally short shrift; he thought it high time an Impressionist exhibition was held in Copenhagen.

Mourier-Petersen presented this sunny canvas, which clearly evinces his affinity with the movement, as a gift to Theo van Gogh. As he wrote from Copenhagen on 25 February 1890, 'Please accept this canvas – *A Field with Tulips* – as a reminder of Christian Mourier-Petersen. May it please you and may the subject remind you of your homeland, even though it was painted in Denmark'.

Christian Vilhelm Mourier-Petersen
Holbaekgaard 1858-1945
A Field with Tulips
Canvas, 34 × 45.5 cm
Inv. S 282 V/1962

Johan Barthold Jongkind
Lattrop 1819-1891 La-Côte-St-André
View near Grenoble
Canvas, 33.1 × 56.2 cm - 1885
Inv. S 411 M/1990

───────────

Though Jongkind was born in Holland he is usually associated with the French seaport of Honfleur and the section of the coast near the towns of Ste-Adresse and Etretat. He immortalised this region as no other artist in the 1860s, during which period he associated with the marine painter Boudin and the young Monet, and profoundly influenced the early development of Impressionism. The last years of his life he spent near Grenoble in La Côte-St-André. Though his art continued to evolve it became uneven. Alcohol took its toll on Jongkind and his touch lost its erstwhile firmness. The situation became so serious that his name was struck from the list of those invited to the Berlioz commemoration at Grenoble in 1885: the organisers feared the painter would imbibe too

much and disrupt the ceremony. Though his watercolours did not suffer notably from his drinking, both the quantity and quality of his painting declined. 1885 was a particularly unproductive year, yet the *View near Grenoble* recalls Jongkind at the height of his powers. Like Guigou – and Van Gogh during his Auvers period – he preferred horizontal formats for landscapes toward the end of his life. Equally striking, however, are the constants in his art: the composition of the illustrated canvas calls to mind the Parisian river views he painted in the 1850s, when he made a name for himself as the 'portraitist of the Seine'. The rafts moored to the bank of the river Isère guide the eye from the foreground into the distance – a device Jongkind had previously employed in a view of the river Schie near Rotterdam. The present view is framed at the left by the imposing Fort Rabot and at the top by the Alps rising above the clouds.

On the whole the chronology of Jongkind's oeuvre is well established. The illustrated view of Grenoble is dated precisely 2 June 1885, which was when the artist sketched the scene on paper, not when he finished the canvas in the studio. In this particular case we even know the composition was constructed from two separate watercolours.
Edmond de Goncourt believed Jongkind's contemporaries under-estimated his significance for Impressionism. As he wrote in 1889, 'Every contemporary landscape of any value is indebted to his skies, his atmosphere, his countryside. It is perfectly obvious, but no one mentions it'.

Before going to Paris Vincent van Gogh had never laid eyes on a picture by an Impressionist, and not until 1886 was he exposed to the art of Monet. This picture must have given him one of his first opportunities to study how Impressionists handled light first hand, since it is one of the many Monets his brother Theo sold in the 1880s. Though the canvas does not appear in the records of Theo's sales, he lent it to an exhibition at the gallery of Georges Petit in the spring of 1887. Its quintessentially Dutch theme must have appealed to Vincent. Besides the light palette, the conspicuously heavy impasto of Monet's picture – which later became so characteristic of Van Gogh's own manner – presumably pleased him as well. Monet returned to the Netherlands in 1886, where he had enjoyed working in the early '70s.

Between 27 April and 6 May 1886 he painted no less than five canvases with bulb fields.
As he wrote from Holland, he found their colours enough 'à rendre fou le pauvre peintre'.

_____

Claude Monet
Paris 1840-1927 Giverny
Bulb Fields and Windmills near Rijnsburg
Canvas, 65 × 81 cm - 1886
Inv. S 40 B/1991, on loan from the
Rijksdienst Beeldende Kunst

Frank Myers Boggs
Springfield 1855-1926 Meudon
The Harbour of Honfleur
Canvas, 38 × 55 cm
Inv. S 212 V/1962

Born in Springfield, Ohio, Boggs studied at the Ecole des Beaux-Arts in Paris in 1876 and thereafter in Gérôme's studio. The French State purchased a work from him as early as 1882. He worked for some time in London in 1883, where he exhibited views of the Thames at the London branch of Goupil's. During a visit to Honfleur in 1884 he painted views of the harbour, just as Jongkind and Boudin had done; the results were shown that same year at the Salon. Vincent van Gogh met Boggs in 1886, the same year Theo sold the American artist a marine by Edouard Manet. Boggs dedicated both of the illustrated pictures 'A son ami' Vincent. In Theo's apartment they hung on either side of a head of a peasant woman from Brabant, and appear in the background of one of Vincent's two portraits of the Scottish art dealer Alexander Reid (now in a private collection).

Boggs is best known for his cityscapes of Paris. On the whole his manner is some-what dryer than these two pictures from the collection of the Van Gogh brothers. Painted in a far more fluent manner, they are obviously indebted to Jongkind. The aforementioned marine by Manet, which Boggs had recently acquired, may have also had some influence on them.

Frank Myers Boggs
Coal Barges on the Thames
Canvas, 38 × 55 cm
Inv. S 213 V/1962

Eugène Boch
La Louvière 1855-1941 Monthyon
The Crachet-Pecry Mine in the Borinage
Canvas, 56 × 78 cm - ca. 1888-90
Inv. S 209 V/1962

The Belgian painter Eugène Boch lived in Paris from 1881, where he had a studio in Montmartre. He studied under Cormon and became a close friend of Bernard, Van Gogh and Toulouse-Lautrec. During the summer of 1888 Boch worked together with the American artist Dodge MacKnight in a small town not far from Arles called Fontvieille. Van Gogh and Boch visited back and forth and Boch sat for his Dutch friend. After leaving Provence,

Boch worked for some years in the Borinage, the Belgian mining district where Van Gogh had taken his first steps on the road to becoming an artist. In October 1888 Vincent wrote Boch that he had never forgotten that 'extraordinary landscape'.
The brothers Van Gogh acquired this picture of the Crachet-Pecry mine in 1890 in exchange for one of Vincent's landscapes of St-Rémy. Theo, who arranged the exchange, described the

canvas enthusiastically in a letter to his brother: 'The entire factory is shrouded in smoke and steam. The bright sunlight makes it stand out strongly against the green wheatfields. The sky is very light [...]. I'd be surprised if you didn't find it at all beautiful'. The Belgian artist's sister Anna Boch was also a painter. She deserves credit for being the first person to purchase a Van Gogh during the artist's lifetime.

　　　BOCH

Arnold Hendrik Koning
Winschoten 1860-1945 Barneveld
Steps in Montmartre
Canvas, 45 × 38 cm
Inv. S 239 V/1962

Arnold Hendrik Koning
Windmill in Montmartre
Canvas, 46 × 38 cm
Inv. S 420 V/1962

Arnold Hendrik Koning
Park with Statues
Canvas laid down on panel, 27 × 40 cm
Inv. S 242 V/1961

After studying at the Rijksacademie in Amsterdam between 1880 and 1885, Arnold Koning moved to Paris in 1886. Together with Anquetin, Bernard, Guillaumin and Toulouse-Lautrec he participated in the exhibition of the 'Impressionnistes du Petit Boulevard' that Van Gogh organised at the Restaurant Du Chalet.

Koning's Parisian cityscapes incorporate some of the same Montmartre motifs found in paintings by Van Gogh. During a second sojourn in the capital in 1888 he lodged with Theo van Gogh, Vincent having just left the city for Arles.

Nowadays the painter and engraver Auguste Lepère is known primarily as a graphic artist; his paintings are rather rare. He started out as an illustrator for such popular magazines as *Le Monde illustré* and *Le Magasin pittoresque*. In his day Lepère was one of the most outspoken proponents of Japonism in graphic art. With its elevated vantage point, this view of Montmartre in winter betrays the artist's knowledge of the method and composition of Japanese printmakers. The dynamic rendering of the small figures is reminiscent of Hiroshige.

How this diminutive canvas entered the collection of the Van Gogh brothers is not known. It may have appealed to Vincent, who painted similar themes during his first Parisian sojourn and kept an eye out for models. The windmill 'le Radet' on the left, also known as the 'Moulin de la Galette', occurs in several of Van Gogh's canvases as well, albeit from an altogether different angle.

Auguste Louis Lepère
Paris 1849-1918 Domme
Montmartre in the Snow
Canvas, 61 × 39 cm
Inv. S 248 V/1962

Albert Wolff (1835-1891), who wrote for *Le Figaro* and authored books extolling Paris as the capital of the arts, penned the following about Rafaëlli: 'Like Millet, he is the poet of humility. What the great master did for the countryside, Raffaëlli has begun to do for simple Parisians'. Renowned authors such as Daudet, Goncourt, Huysmans and Zola contributed to Raffaëlli's album *Les Types de Paris*, published by *Le Figaro* in 1889. Raffaëlli's portrayal of city workers likewise won the admiration of Vincent van Gogh. The urban equivalent of the Dutch artist's hero Jean-François Millet, Raffaëlli exhibited in 1890 at the gallery managed by Theo van Gogh. His self-portrait of 1879 – the only one known by the artist – is based in part on a photograph. Utilising various types of pastel and black chalk, the artist combined techniques normally associated with painting and drawing, as the critic Edmond Duranty had recommended in his influential brochure *La Nouvelle Peinture*. The Frenchman even went so far as to patent the method. The palette betrays his indebtedness to his friend Degas, who had ensured his participation in various exhibitions of the Impressionists, though Raffaëlli's highly expressive manner distinguishes from his far more detached colleague.

Raffaëlli exhibited his self-portrait in a one-man show in the spring of 1884. The catalogue includes an essay by the artist entitled 'Etude des mouvements de l'art moderne et du beau caractériste', in which he defined his position *vis-à-vis* Realism, Impressionism and Naturalism. Van Gogh read the essay in 1885 and was moved by the 'mixture of very simple words that come from the heart and from a nervous artistic sensibility'. *The Veterans* is an example of Raffaëlli at his most attractive. The sober palette is enlivened only by the red decoration on the lapel of the man at the right. The daring obstruction of the central figure may have been inspired by Degas.

Jean-François Raffaëlli
Lyons 1850-1924 Paris
Self-portrait
Pastel, 54 × 39 cm - 1879
Inv. D 1034 V/1992

Jean-François Raffaëlli
The Veterans
Panel, 56.8 × 39.9 cm
Inv. S 415 M/1990

Armand Guillaumin
Paris 1841-1927 Crozaut
Portrait of a Young Woman
Canvas, 65 × 54 cm
Inv. S 227 V/1961

Armand Guillaumin was one of the first
Impressionists. Van Gogh admired him
very much, as indicated by the letter he
wrote his sister Wil on 19 September
1889: 'I recently made two self-portraits,

one of which captures the character
rather well I think, but in Holland they'd
probably scoff at the ideas about
portraits that are developing here.
'Did you see the portrait at Theo's of the

painter Guillaumin and that of a young woman by the same artist? When Guillaumin exhibited the portrait, public and artists alike had a good laugh, yet it's one of the very few things that could bear comparison to the old Dutch masters, even to Rembrandt and Hals'.

Henri de Toulouse-Lautrec
Albi 1864-1901 Malromé
Portrait of Vincent van Gogh
Pastel on cardboard, 57 × 46.5 cm - 1887
Inv. D 693 V/1962

Vincent van Gogh became acquainted with Henri de Toulouse-Lautrec in 1886 in the studio of Fernand Cormon, where both men were studying. It was through Cormon that Vincent also met Emile Bernard and Louis Anquetin. A scion of an old aristocratic family from Languedoc, Toulouse-Lautrec took lessons from the horse painter René Princeteau before deciding to pursue an artistic career in 1882. As well as in Cormon's he studied in Bonnat's studio, and was influenced by Bastien-Lepage, whose reputation was then at its zenith. He found his themes in brothels, music halls and cabarets such as the Moulin de la Galette and Le Mirliton, thus earning himself the sobriquet 'the Utamaro of Montmartre'. This pastel portrait with its bold palette attests to the affinity between Toulouse-Lautrec and Van Gogh. The latter is seen in profile against the background of one of the many cafés where so much of the French capital's effervescent artistic life took place. In his *Souvenirs*, Emile Bernard claims his friend was seated in the Café du Tambourin, but it could just as easily have been one of those on the Avenue de Clichy. On the table stands a glass of absinthe, the notorious brew that ruined so many artists, Toulouse-Lautrec himself being among its most famous victims. Indeed Van Gogh devoted one of his most charming Parisian still lifes to the noxious drink. The composition of that canvas recalls another work by Toulouse-Lautrec, *The Billiard Room*, dated 1882 (Musée Toulouse-Lautrec, Albi); it, too, shows a carafe and a glass of absinthe. The view of the street adds an extra dimension to Van Gogh's small canvas, while the slant of the windows betrays the influence of Japanese graphic art.

Vincent van Gogh
Zundert 1853-1890 Auvers-sur-Oise
A Glass of Absinthe and a Carafe
Canvas, 46.5 × 33 cm - 1887
Inv. S 186 V/1962 - F 339

Henri de Toulouse-Lautrec
Albi 1864-1901 Malromé
Two Prostitutes in a Café
Panel, 24 × 17 cm - 1885/1886
Inv. S 275 V/1962

The popularity among Impressionists of the theme of a woman sitting alone in a café can be traced to Edgar Degas's *L'Absinthe* of 1876 (Paris, Musée d'Orsay). Though we cannot be altogether certain that this portrait of a young woman by Toulouse-Lautrec is in fact set in a café, the canvas certainly belongs to the same tradition. The small red jar in front of her is of the kind that held scented rice powder, which women used to make themselves appear fashionably pale. The sitter is probably Suzanna Valadon, the artist's mistress at the time. The style is patently influenced by Neo-impressionism.

Toulouse-Lautrec made his debut in 1888 at the exhibition of Les XX in Brussels with *Poudre de riz*. Theo van Gogh had purchased the picture on 12 January of that year, just prior to his brother's departure for Arles. When Vincent later painted his famous portrait of Patience Escalier in the Rhône city, he suggested that Theo hang the two works side by side: 'I don't think my peasant would do any harm to your Lautrec. Indeed I would go so far as to say the contrast will make it look even more distinguished, and that mine will gain by the odd juxtaposition. The sun-baked, tanned quality, browned by the sun and air, will stand out better beside the rice powder and the elegance'.

The small panel by Toulouse-Lautrec showing two prostitutes in a café also belonged to the brothers Van Gogh. Compared to the woman in *Poudre de riz*, there is something caricature-like about the two figures in this virtually monochromatic work.

Henri de Toulouse-Lautrec
Young Woman at a Table (Poudre de riz)
Canvas, 56 × 46 cm - 1887
Inv. S 274 V/1962

109

Louis Anquetin
Etrépagny 1861-1932 Paris
Old Peasant
Canvas, 120 × 90 cm - 1886. Inv. S 384 M/1988

Louis Anquetin
Night Sail
(Bateau, la nuit)
*Pastel, 49.5 × 64.5 cm -
1887*
Inv. D 1035 V/1992

Anquetin was a close friend of Toulouse-Lautrec and Laval, whom he got to know in Bonnat's studio; Bernard and Van Gogh he met later in Cormon's. Anquetin was among those who exhibited their work at the Restaurant du Grand Bouillon on the Avenue de Clichy in November 1887, along with the other 'Impressionnistes du Petit Boulevard'. He is credited with the invention of Cloisonnism, the style that was to have such an impact on Bernard, Gauguin and Van Gogh.
Stylistically the *Old Peasant* of 1886 still has much in common with the Impressionism of Monet, whom Anquetin greatly admired. Particularly daring is the almost photographic manner in which the old man, leaning on two canes – just as the young fruit tree at the left is protected by two strips of barbed wire – is seen against the light.

The canvas may possibly be identical with the study *Le Paysan*, mentioned by Van Gogh in a letter to Bernard of 15 July 1888 and sold by the dealer Georges ('Père') Thomas.

In late 1887 Louis Anquetin exhibited a picture entitled *Bateau, soleil couchant* at Van Gogh's first exhibition of the 'Impressionnistes du Petit Boulevard'. The work has since vanished without a trace. Contemporaries were struck by the artist's brazen use of the colour red, which dominated the work. In keeping with Cloisonnism, the forms were simplified and in accordance with the chromatic theories of the Neo-impressionists the colours were charged with symbolic meaning. Anquetin exhibited the seascape once more that winter at the offices of *La Revue indépendante*, then at the fifth

exhibition of Les XX in Brussels and finally – between March and May 1888 – at the Salon des Indépendants. The illustrated pastel *Bateau, la nuit*, which must be closely related to the red picture, is dominated by another colour – blue – symbolising the night. The yellow of the stars and the foam of the waves form the only contrasts.
The motif of a ship on a turbulent sea is pre-eminently Romantic, but Realists such as Courbet and Millet were also fond of it. Japanese prints may have had some influence on Anquetin's decorative pastel as well. Indeed Edouard Dujardin, the influential critic who wrote for *La Revue indépendante*, acclaimed Anquetin the most important 'Japoniste' of the group of young Cloisonnists. Van Gogh, however, objected. In his opinion it was Bernard who deserved the compliment.

Emile Bernard
Lille 1868-1941 Paris
Two Breton Women in a Meadow
Panel, 62 × 82 cm - 1886
Inv. S 437 M/1992

The name of Emile Bernard has figured prominently in the preceding pages. From the moment they met in Cormon's studio, there was an obvious affinity between Bernard and Van Gogh. Indeed the sole surviving photograph of Vincent from his Parisian period shows him with Bernard on the bank of the Seine near Asnières, where the two artists often worked.

When he met Van Gogh, Bernard was not yet established, but he would soon play a stimulating role within the Parisian avant-garde. After his Dutch friend left Paris in 1888 the two corresponded regularly.

His letters to Bernard inform us a great deal about Van Gogh's views on art. After Vincent's death Bernard took pains to ensure the critical recognition of his 'copaign'. The occasional inaccuracy notwithstanding, he recorded much about Van Gogh in Paris that would otherwise have been lost.

Emile Bernard
Rag Collector Fishing
Canvas, 38.8 × 51.5 cm - ca. 1886/87
Inv. S 367 V/1982

In about 1886 Bernard went through a brief Neo-impressionist phase. His first exposure to the work of Seurat and Signac may have already occurred at the second Salon de la Société des Artistes Indépendants of that year. But when, around April-May 1887, Bernard changed course under the influence of Anquetin, he disavowed the movement and sought to eradicate every trace of his 'error'. This Breton landscape was painted during the summer of 1886 and once belonged to Theo van Gogh's brother-in-law Andries Bonger; it shows that by the time he rejected Neo-impressionism, Bernard had developed his own variation on Seurat's stippling. Though painted in a predominantly Impressionist mode, *Rag Collector Fishing* also betrays Seurat's influence. It is difficult to imagine Bernard choosing the theme or painting the figure's silhouette without first having seen the abstracted figures in Seurat's famous *A Sunday Afternoon on the Island of La Grande-Jatte* (1886). The asymmetry of the composition is patently Japanese. Louis Anquetin's pastel of his fellow student Emile Bernard was first thought to be the latter's self-portrait. The sheet may have been a study for a larger, more ambitious composition of a café scene, for which Bernard happened to model; this would explain the conspicuous grid.

Louis Anquetin
Portrait of Emile Bernard
Pastel, 71 × 59 cm - ca. 1887
Inv. D 914 M/1990, presented by Elin Ekström

Emile Bernard
Lille 1868-1941 Paris
Vase with Flowers and Bowl
Canvas, 40 × 32 cm - ca. 1887
Inv. S 255 V/1962

Bernard's parents were not pleased to learn of their son's artistic aspirations. During the ensuing struggle, which lasted for many years, only his maternal grandmother, Sophie Bodin-Lallement, supported him.

It was she who financed the construction of a modest atelier for the aspiring artist in the garden of his parents' house in Asnières.

The characteristic features of Madame Bodin figure repeatedly in Bernard's work of the 1880s, and nowhere more suggestively than in this canvas, painted during the autumn of 1887.

The picture of an old Arlésienne that Van Gogh made in early 1888 was inspired by this portrait of his friend's grandmother. Vincent described Bernard's portrait in a letter to his sister Wil, penned much later, in December 1889: 'a very old woman with one eye. The background is formed by the wall of a room with chocolate-coloured wallpaper and a bed done completely in white'.

Van Gogh was only mistaken about the 'wallpaper', for the folds in the floral pattern betray the fact that a cloth was suspended in the background.

Vincent knew the portrait very well. Not only did he include it in the exhibition he organised of the 'Impressionnistes du Petit Boulevard' at the Restaurant du Chalet, but he also gave Bernard one of his own self-portraits in exchange for it. In August 1888, unhappy with the direction Bernard's work was taking, he reminded his friend of the still lifes and the portraits of his grandmother he had previously painted: 'Have you ever made anything better, and have you ever been more *yourself*, more of a personality?' Their quality lay in 'the indescribable wilfulness, great wisdom, the ineffable austerity, power and self-assurance that they emanated. Never,

dear friend, have you come closer to
Rembrandt than you did then'. The
portrait clearly betrays the influence of
Japanese graphic art, which Bernard had
learned to appreciate through Van Gogh.
Besides the portrait of his grandmother,
the Dutch artist numbered his young
colleague's still lifes among those

'manly things' of which Bernard could
be proud. The small composition
illustrated here, showing flowers and a
bowl with oriental decoration, was
probably created in two stages.
In the autumn of 1887 Bernard overpainted an earlier, more Impressionist
version with areas of more solid colour.

The curious vase is reminiscent of
Cézanne's famous *Vase Bleue* in the
Musée d'Orsay.
Bernard could have seen work by
Cézanne at the paint dealer Père
Tanguy's, whose portrait he painted at
about the same time as that of his
grandmother.

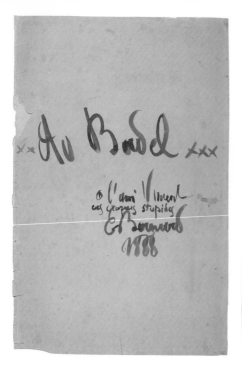

In early October 1888 Bernard sent Van Gogh a dozen drawings in Arles, inscribed with the words 'These stupid scribbles are for my friend Vincent'. Scenes from a brothel form the motif and the series is introduced by a poem. The drawings introduce us to a world generally associated with Bernard's colleague Toulouse-Lautrec. Probably executed in Paris in September 1888, they are all inscribed with a short, ironic caption. Van Gogh found Bernard's poem 'masterly', but was critical of some of the drawings. He liked the woman washing in particular, but some of the

Emile Bernard
Lille 1868-1941 Paris
Title page and 11 illustrations entitled 'Au Bordel'
Watercolour, each ca. 40.4 × 27 cm
Inv. D 624-34 V/1962

prostitutes 'smirked' too much and were
'too pale, not fleshy enough' for his taste.
Yet the Dutchman had no doubts about
the theme: 'Au bordel. Yes, that's the
sort of thing we should be making [...]'.

Claude-Emile Schuffenecker
Fresne-St-Mamès 1851-1934 Paris
Portrait of Count Antoine de la Rochefoucauld
Canvas, 69.8 × 56.2 cm - 1884/86
Inv. S 430 M/1992

Emile Schuffenecker's artistic development was manifestly influenced by almost every important artistic current in the course of the 1880s. He succumbed successively to Impressionism, Neo-impressionism and Symbolism. In this portrait the artist seems uncertain as to which style to adopt. While the portrait itself is characteristically Impressionist, the background is vaguely Neo-impressionist.

The sitter is said to be Antoine de la Rochefoucauld, a wealthy aristocrat who – himself a poet and a painter – moved in Symbolist circles in the late 1880s. Rochefoucauld underwrote the first Salon de la Rose+Croix in 1892 and supported the painters Bernard, Filiger and Sérusier.

Paul Signac, friend of Seurat and tireless defender of Neo-impressionism, started out as an admirer of Monet. His earliest Impressionist work also betrays the influence of Armand Guillaumin, whom he had got to know in 1884. It was Jean-François Raffaëlli who interested Signac in painting the suburbs of Paris. He was the first artist of any stature whom Van Gogh befriended in the capital, and though of course it was he who introduced the Dutchman to Neo-impressionism, at first Vincent was more impressed by the Frenchman's erstwhile Impressionism.

In his depiction of the station of Asnières, Signac seems to eschew anything remotely picturesque: a telegraph pole slices unabashedly through the foreground, nor is there a single motif that would seem worth the paint. His friend's rough handling of such prosaic elements evidently fascinated Van Gogh, to judge from the truncated poles and carelessly rendered fencing that occur in his own Parisian work. At the Impressionists' last group show in 1886, when Seurat exhibited his pioneering *Un dimanche sur l'Ile de la Grande-Jatte*, Signac displayed fifteen of his own works, including a new version of this picture with the railway yard of Bois Colombes. The broad, expressive strokes he had treated the motif with in 1885 gave way to the *pointille* of Neo-impressionism.

In the spring of 1887 Signac left Paris for the south of France. He stayed in touch with Van Gogh, however, even after his friend moved to Arles. Yet Vincent declined a subsequent invitation to exhibit with Signac on the grounds that their artistic paths had diverged.

Paul Signac
Paris 1863-1935 Paris
Railroad Crossing near the Station Bois
Colombes in Asnières
Canvas, 46.4 × 65 cm - 1885
Inv. S 381 M/1986

Léo Gausson
Lagny-sur-Marne 1860-1944 Lagny-sur-Marne
The Church Tower of Bussy-St-Georges,
Seine-et-Marne
Canvas, 46 × 55 cm - 1887/88
Inv. S 226 V/1962

From a stylistic point of view, Gausson
was nearly as mercurial as
Schuffenecker. He, too, went through
many styles in rapid succession, becoming known as the 'travelling salesman
in avant-garde'. Yet the illustrated
village view is an example of pure Neo-
impressionism, clearly influenced by
Gausson's friend Lucien Pissarro.
On 5 June 1890 Gausson wrote Theo
van Gogh that he wished to exchange
one of his own works for one of his
brother's. Despite the delay caused by
Vincent's subsequent death, the
exchange was posthumously effected
following Gausson's second request in
August. Though the two artists never
met, Gausson had admired Van Gogh's
work at Père Tanguy's.

119

Claude-Emile Schuffenecker
Fresne-St-Mamès 1851-1934 Paris
Landscape with Resting Figure
Canvas, 59.5 × 73.2 cm - 1888
Inv. S 379 M/1986

Gauguin's Pont-Aven. At the time he painted the sun-drenched *Landscape with Resting Figure*, Schuffenecker was evidently more attracted to the Impressionism of Claude Monet than to the new Symbolism and Synthetism coming out of Pont-Aven, whereas the somewhat later *Cliffs by the Coast of Brittany* is more Symbolist.

In both of the exhibited landscapes someone is seen walking. The motif of a figure seen from the back, sunk in contemplation before a landscape, was dear to the Romantics. Several Impressionists also tried their hand at it, since it afforded the opportunity to include a landscape and the experience of it in one and the same canvas. Schuffenecker's figure – wearing a straw hat known as a *canotier*, and inevitably accompanied by a dog – explicitly alludes to the artist's own view of nature. The Frenchman once described his ideal landscape as the realisation of the 'dream of the Garden of Eden'.

Schuffenecker started out in banking, but studied art in his free time with the leading painters Baudry and Carolus Duran. He also encouraged his colleague Paul Gauguin to pursue an artistic career. Together they frequented the Impressionists Guillaumin and Pissarro. Schuffenecker exhibited at the Salons of 1880 and '81, but following his rejection in '83, he took part in the first Salon des Indépendants in '84. While Gauguin was in Panama and Martinique, Schuffenecker acted as his agent. Later on he also lent his friend financial assistance and even took him under his roof – until, that is, the indiscreet Gauguin started making overtures to his wife. Thenceforth relations between the two men cooled, though Schuffenecker continued to look after Gauguin's affairs from time to time.

Like Gauguin, Schuffenecker spent much time working in Brittany, but preferred the village of Concarneau to

In 1889 Schuffenecker organised an exhibition on the grounds of the Exposition Universelle in Paris. He

Claude-Emile Schuffenecker
Peasant Boy Seated
Pastel, 27.9 × 43.2 cm
Inv. D 803 V/1982

managed to interest a certain Volpini who owned a café that happened to be ideally located. Provocatively entitled 'Groupe Impressionniste et Synthétiste', the show included works by Anquetin, Bernard, Gauguin, Laval and Schuffenecker himself. Nevertheless Theo van Gogh refused to lend six canvases by his brother, much to Vincent's chagrin. Though Schuffenecker and Van Gogh were not particularly close, the latter's correspondence is sprinkled with references to 'le bon Schuff'. By the same token, we are indebted to Gauguin's letters to Schuffenecker for much information about Van Gogh. Schuffenecker was one of the earliest collectors of Van Gogh's work, and – together with his brother Amedée – one of the first to deal in it, as well.

Paul Gauguin
Paris 1848-1903 Atuana
On the Bank of the Lake in Martinique
Canvas, 54 × 65 cm - 1887
Inv. S 220 V/1962

Gauguin's father was a French journalist, his mother Creole. Having started out in the merchant marine, he subsequently became a stockbroker. The Impressionists' first exhibition in 1874 inspired him to become a painter and only two years later he showed a landscape in the style of Pissarro at the Salon. Gauguin collected work by Manet, Monet and other Impressionists and participated in their group shows between 1880 and 1882. Despite the speed with which he mastered his craft, at first he had difficulty selling his own art.

By the spring of 1887 Gauguin was in such dire financial straits that he decided to seek his fortune elsewhere.

In April he and his friend Charles Laval set out for Panama. To earn some money Gauguin spent two weeks working on the Panama Canal, after which the twosome moved on to Martinique, where their boat had anchored briefly on the voyage out. With its amiable population, this paradisical Caribbean island was more like what Gauguin had imagined. The artists rented a cabin near the port of St-Pierre, but within four months dysentery, a liver ailment and fever drove Gauguin back to Paris. By the time he left Martinique Gauguin had painted a dozen pictures, two of which found their way into the hands of Theo and Vincent van Gogh. According to one of Vincent's letters to his sister, he acquired the illustrated landscape from the artist in exchange for one of his own canvases. He described the work as 'a dried up river with purple mud, puddles of water that reflect the pure cobalt blue of the sky, and green grass. A negro boy with a white and red cow, a negro woman in blue and some green woods'.

As for Gauguin's travelling companion, Charles Laval studied under Bonnat and Cormon, in whose studios he befriended Anquetin and Toulouse-Lautrec. After returning from Martinique Laval rejoined the circle of painters round Gauguin in Pont-Aven. Given the stylistic similarity of Laval's landscape to Gauguin's, no wonder it has been attributed to his friend. In 1888 Laval exchanged his *Self-portrait* for a work by Van Gogh, who described it as 'very powerful and very distinguished' and was especially struck by 'the gaze through the eyeglass, such a sincere gaze'. Laval attended Vincent's funeral in 1890. Four years later he himself died of tuberculosis in Egypt. Shortly before his death he married Emile Bernard's sister Madeleine.

Charles Laval
1862-Cairo 1894
Landscape in Martinique
Canvas, 60 × 73.5 cm - 1887
Inv. S 378 V/1982

Charles Laval
Self-portrait
Canvas, 50 × 60 cm - 1888
Inv. S 247 V/1962

Paul Gauguin
Paris 1848-1903 Atuana
Head of a Girl from Martinique
Coloured chalk, 36 × 27 cm - 1887
Inv. D 664 V/1962

Paul Gauguin
Under the Mangoes in Martinique
Canvas, 89 × 116 cm - 1887
Inv. S 221 V/1962

The brothers Van Gogh became acquainted with the work of Gauguin through their neighbour in Paris, the paint dealer Alphonse Portier. In January 1888, shortly before his brother left for Arles, Theo exhibited three paintings and five pieces of pottery by Gauguin in his gallery.
Vincent described *Under the Mangoes in Martinique* to his sister Wil in July 1888: 'Theo bought a large picture from him [i.e. Gauguin] at the time, showing negresses dressed in pink, blue, orange and yellow cotton under the tamarind, palm and banana trees, with the sea in the distance'. He compared the theme to Pierre Lot's book *Le mariage* and described the canvas to Bernard as 'edifying poetry'.
Under the Mangoes is indubitably the finest picture Gauguin painted on Martinique. It was the first step in his search for the paradisiacal and the primitive, a search that would occupy him for the rest of his life.
The figure of the large negress recurs in a fan-shaped gouache with Martinique motifs that once belonged to the composer Ernest Chausson (now in the National Museum for Western Art, Tokyo).
Few of the works Gauguin executed on paper in Martinique survive. The lovely girl in this colourful pastel is a worthy forerunner of the exotic beauties the artist later painted on Tahiti.

Along with Cézanne, Degas, Guillaumin, Monet, Renoir and Sisley, Camille Pissarro was one of the first Impressionists. He exhibited not only at the Salon des Refusés of 1863, but also at all eight of the famous Impressionist exhibitions between 1874 and 1886. In 1886 Pissarro met Seurat and became the first Impressionist to make the transition to Neo-impressionism, even before Signac in other words. Pissarro's conversion was crucial to the movement, which was still in its infancy at the time. His insistence that it was the logical sequel to Impressionism greatly enhanced its credibility. Pissarro saw himself as a 'scientific' Impressionist at this point, and labelled his former colleagues scornfully as Romantics. Pissarro's change of heart did not help his relationship with his dealer Durand-Ruel. Theo van Gogh helped the artist through the financial consequences. The two men had met during the summer of 1887, the same year Vincent van Gogh exchanged work with Pissarro's son Lucien, who was an artist as well. In gratitude for his support, Pissarro gave Theo two fan-shaped gouaches on 12 December 1889. In the accompanying letter he wrote 'A land-scape with rainbow is for Madame van Gogh, and I would like to ask you to be so kind as to present this to her on my behalf, along with my best wishes for the New Year'. Theo promptly informed Vincent of the gift of the 'bien joli éventail'. Fans also figured in the exhibition of Pissarro's work that Theo organised at his gallery in 1890, where they were acclaimed by the critic Gustave Geoffroy: 'the light becomes even brighter, softening the calm fields, the spacious skies and the pure horizons'. By the time he painted the fan for Johanna van Gogh, Pissarro had already begun to distance himself from

the art of Seurat. Yet apparently he did not throw the principles of Divisionism entirely overboard: since the *pointilles* had cost him too much time, he now adopted his own, somewhat looser manner, distinguished by small stripes or dashes, so as to combine 'the purity, the simplicity of the *pointille* and the softness, suppleness, freedom,

spontaneity and freshness of our Impressionist art'. Yet the rainbow that dominates the present composition would still seem to be an unequivocal homage to the principle of Divisionism, or the separation of colours, which had so occupied Pissarro in recent years that he had been willing to risk his financial security for it.

Camille Pissaro
St-Thomas-des-Antilles 1830-1903 Paris
Figures in a Meadow
Coloured chalk, 30 × 60 cm - 1889
Inv. D 685 V/1962

Vincent van Gogh
Window in the Restaurant Chez Bataille in Paris
Pen and ink, coloured chalk on blue paper,
53.5 × 39.5 cm - 1887
Inv. D 350 V/1962 - F 1392

Van Gogh in Paris

Fragment of a letter from Van Gogh, written in Paris between August and October 1886, to the English painter Horace M. Livens, whom he had met in Antwerp.

'[...] I intend remaining here still longer. There is much to be seen here – for instance Delacroix, to name only one master. In Antwerp I did not even know what the impressionists were, now I have seen them and though *not* being one of the club yet I have much admired certain impressionists' pictures – *Degas* nude figure – *Claude Monet* landscape. 'And now for what regards what I myself have been doing, I have lacked money for paying models else I had entirely given myself to figure painting. But I have made a series of colour studies in painting simply flowers [...]. 'Now after these gymnastics I lately did two heads which I dare say are better in light and colour than those I did before. So as we said at the time: in *colour* seeking *life* the true drawing is modelling with colour. I did a dozen landscapes too, frankly *green*, frankly *blue*. And so I am struggling for life and progress in art [...].

'As regards my chances of selling, look, they're certainly not great but still *I have made* a beginning. At present I've found four dealers who've exhibited studies of mine, and I've exchanged studies with many artists. [...] I was in Cormon's studio for three or four months but didn't find that as useful as I'd expected it to be. But that may be my fault. Anyhow I left there too, just as I left Antwerp. Since then I've been working alone and fancy that I feel more like myself'.

Vincent van Gogh
Plaster Torso and Notes
Blue and black chalk on sketchbook sheet
20.3 × 13 cm - 1886
Inv. D 140 V/1962 - FSD 1716 r

In early March 1886 Van Gogh had gone to Paris unexpectedly to study in Fernand Cormon's atelier. His Parisian sojourn lasted exactly two years and effectively transformed his work. By the time he left he had become acquainted with both Impressionism and Neo-impressionism. Through his brother Theo, with whom he lodged, he made numerous contacts in the art world. His friendship with Anquetin, Bernard, Signac and Toulouse-Lautrec gave him access to the avant-garde.

Vincent van Gogh
Plaster Statuette of a Female Torso
Pasteboard, 46 × 38 cm
Inv. S 56 V/1962 - F 216a

Vincent van Gogh
Plaster Cast of a Torso
Pasteboard, 46.5 × 38 cm
Inv. S 89 V/1962 - F 216b

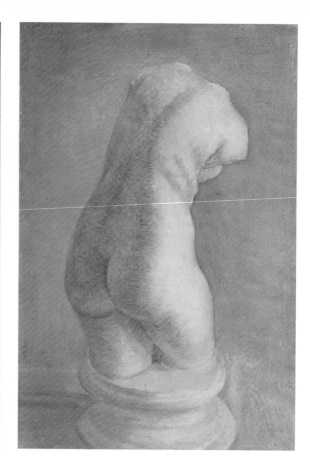

Vincent van Gogh
Plaster Cast of a Torso
Canvas, 40.5 × 27 cm
Inv. S 199 V/1962 - F 216g

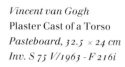

Vincent van Gogh
Plaster Cast of a Torso
Pasteboard, 32.5 × 24 cm
Inv. S 75 V/1963 - F 216i

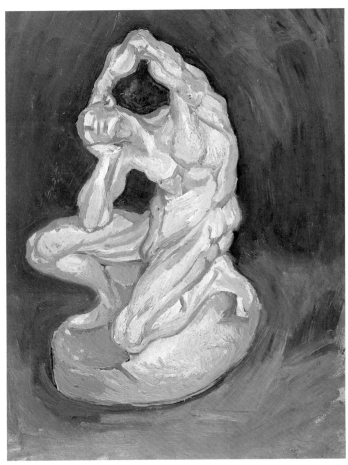

Vincent van Gogh
Plaster Cast of a
Kneeling Man
Pasteboard, 35 × 27 cm
Inv. S 102 V/1962 - F 216f

Vincent van Gogh
Plaster Cast of a Torso
Pasteboard, 35 × 27 cm
Inv. S 103 V/1962 - F 216e

Vincent van Gogh
Plaster Cast of a Horse
Pasteboard, 33 × 41 cm
Inv. S 202 V/1962 - F 216c

One of Van Gogh's motives for going to
Paris was to pursue his artistic training
in Fernand Cormon's atelier. Though
the exact dates of his attendance are not
known, he presumably reported soon
after his arrival in the French capital,
and spent a total of three or four
months. Most of the time he worked
from live models or plaster casts.
Besides countless study drawings, he
also produced an attractive series of oil
studies after plaster casts against a blue
background. Several of the original
casts are preserved in the Museum.
Cormon's studio proved to be a
breeding ground for the avant-garde.
It was there that Van Gogh met Emile
Bernard, Louis Anquetin, Henri de
Toulouse-Lautrec and the Australian
Impressionist John Russell, for
instance.

Vincent van Gogh
Self-portrait with Dark Felt Hat
Canvas, 41.5 × 32.5 cm - 1886
Inv. S 162 V/1962 - F 208a

Vincent van Gogh
Self-portrait with Pipe
Canvas, 46 × 38 cm - 1886
Inv. S 158 V/1962 - F 180

Vincent van Gogh
Self-portrait with
Pipe
Canvas, 27 × 19 cm -
1886
Inv. S 159 V/1962 -
F 208

Of the many self-portraits Van Gogh painted, no less than eighteen of which are in the Van Gogh Museum, most date from his Parisian period.

It was in Antwerp that he decided to become a portraitist. Like Rembrandt early in his career, he turned to self-portraiture as an inexpensive method of studying the effects of light.

The three self-portraits illustrated here are among the earliest Vincent is known to have painted in Paris. As yet there seems to be no trace of the profound self-analysis many have read into these canvases. They are still distinguished by the dark palette of his Nuenen period and a Rembrandtesque incidence of light. In his dress, however, we see him break new ground: whereas in Brabant he had usually worn a peasant blouse, here he sports a felt hat apparently in an attempt to identify himself as a city dweller.

Living with his brother, he must have felt a certain obligation to adapt to Theo's circle of friends, and indeed Archibald S. Hartrick, with whom Vincent studied in Paris, recalled in *A Painter's Pilgrimage through Fifty Years* that he 'dressed quite well and in an ordinary way, better than many in the atelier'. The two self-portraits with the pipe seem somewhat later than that with the felt hat.

Vincent van Gogh
The Hill of Montmartre with Quarry
Canvas, 56.2 × 62.5 cm - 1886
Inv. S 12 V/1962 - F 230

Vincent van Gogh
Sloping Path on Montmartre
Pasteboard, 22 × 16 cm - 1886
Inv. S 92 V/1963 - F 232

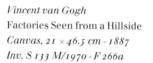

Vincent van Gogh
Factories Seen from a Hillside
Canvas, 21 × 46.5 cm - 1887
Inv. S 133 M/1970 - F 266a

Montmartre had long been popular with artists. In Hendrik Willem Mesdag's collection in The Hague, Van Gogh had had the opportunity to admire two pictures with windmills in the suburb by Georges Michel (1763-1843), and he himself owned a print with Montmartre subjects by August Delâtre, which probably influenced his choice of themes. Van Gogh made the fresh outdoor study of the quarry in the autumn of 1886. His fellow countryman Matthijs Maris had previously painted it in the early 1870s (Gemeentemuseum, The Hague). Though the windmill just to the right of centre plays a relatively minor role within the composition, its placement at the intersection of the dramatic bank of clouds and the fence running diagonally over the hill focuses our attention on it. The Blute-Fin, as the mill was called, formed the subject of many other pictures Van Gogh painted during this period.

In June 1886 Vincent and Theo van Gogh moved into a flat in Rue Lepic, located on the Butte Montmartre. During his first stay in Paris in 1875/76 Van Gogh had lived in the same quarter. This period witnessed the suburb's gradual absorption by the burgeoning metropolis and its hey-day as a centre of entertainment. Despite these changes, Montmartre retained some of its rural charm, which fascinated Vincent, even if he occasionally included the factories in his work.

Vincent van Gogh
View of the Roofs of Paris
Canvas, 54 × 72.5 cm - 1886
Inv. S 13 V/1962 - F 261

The manner of these early Parisian views is still tonal, and more closely related to Corot and the Barbizon School than to the Impressionists. Vincent became acquainted with the latter at this time, but had not yet been converted to their particular vision.

On 10 July 1887 Theo van Gogh wrote his friend Caro van Stockum-Haanebeek in The Hague about the recent changes in his domestic life. 'As you may know I am living with my brother Vincent, who is studying painting with inexhaustible zeal. Since he needs a fair amount of space for his work, we are living in a rather large flat in Montmartre which, as you know, is built against a hill on the outskirts of Paris. The most remarkable thing about it is the splendid view of the city from one of the windows, with the hills of Meudon, St Cloud and so forth on the horizon, and a piece of sky almost as large as when one stands on the dunes. 'With all the effects the changing sky produces, it's a theme for I don't know how many pictures. If you saw it you'd add that it is even suitable for poetry'.

Vincent van Gogh
Vase with Forget-Me-Nots and Peonies
Pasteboard, 34.5 × 27.5 cm - summer 1886
Inv. S 182 V/1962 - F 243a

Vincent van Gogh
Glass with Roses
Pasteboard, 35 × 27 cm - summer 1886
Inv. S 178 V/1962 - F 218

Vincent van Gogh
Coleus in a Flowerpot
Canvas, 42 × 22 cm - summer 1886
Inv. S 185 V/1962 - F 281

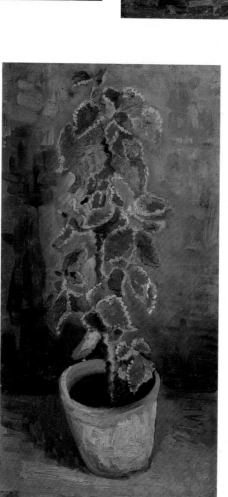

The fact that most of the flower still lifes Vincent painted in Paris are unsigned indicates that they were originally colour studies. In late July 1886 Theo wrote their mother that Vincent's friends regularly supplied him with fresh flowers that summer for these 'finger exercises'. In a letter about his first months in Paris to the English painter Horace Mann Livens, whom he had met in Antwerp, Vincent wrote: 'I have lacked money for paying models else I had entirely given myself to figure painting. But I have made a series of colour studies in painting, simply flowers, red poppies, blue corn flowers and forget-me-nots, white and pink roses, yellow chrysanthemums – looking for contrasts between blue and orange, red and green, yellow and violet for *les tons rompus et neutres* to harmonise brutal extremes. Trying to achieve intense *colour* and not *grey* harmony'.

While living in Brabant Van Gogh immersed himself in colour theory by reading Charles Blanc's *Grammaire des arts du dessin*. Though he had previously painted a few flower still lifes in Nuenen, in Paris he had the opportunity to test his theoretical knowledge against the practice of other still-life painters. Theo himself owned flower pieces by Jeannin and Fantin-Latour; as well as a watercolour with grapes and pears by Sientje Mesdag-van Houten, these are now in the Van Gogh Museum. At the Salon of 1886, moreover, Vincent admired the work of the flower painter Ernest Quost. But the Provençal painter Adolphe Monticelli, one of whose flower still lifes was in the Van Gogh brothers' collection, had the greatest impact on him by far. In February 1890, after Albert Aurier had praised Van Gogh as 'the only painter who observes colour

gradations with that intensity, with that sharpness of metal and precious stones', Vincent modestly referred the critic to this picture in Theo's collection, 'a certain bouquet by Monticelli – a bouquet in white, forget-me-not blue and orange'.

Van Gogh's impasto is often traced to Monticelli. Yet these still lifes also recall a painting by Manet that Vincent and Theo had seen at the Parisian auction house of Drouot: a bouquet of 'large pink peonies with their green leaves against a light background', painted 'in thick impastos and not built up from layers of transparent paint, like those of Jeannin'. The work by Manet seems to have inspired many a flower piece by Van Gogh.

The still life *Mussels and Shrimps* calls to mind a rather pathetic anecdote in Gauguin's posthumously published

Avant et Après. The Frenchman recounts how, in the winter of 1886, a numb and hungry Van Gogh walked into a junk shop on Rue Lepic to sell 'a small still life – pink shrimps on a pink background', so that he could buy food. 'Poor artist!' wrote Gauguin. 'You've invested part of your soul in the small canvas you've come to sell'. No sooner had the dealer given him 100 sous for it, than the impecunious painter handed the money to a beggar who chanced to pass at that moment.

Vincent van Gogh
Mussels and Shrimps
*Canvas, 26.5 × 34.5 cm -
autumn 1886
Inv. S 122 V/1962 - F 256*

Vincent van Gogh
Vase with Asters and Phlox
Canvas, 61 × 46 cm - summer 1886
Inv. S 177 V/1962 - F 234

Vincent van Gogh
Vase with Gladioli
Canvas, 46.5 × 38.5 cm - summer 1886
Inv. S 144 V/1962 - F 248a

Vincent van Gogh
Boulevard de Clichy, Paris
Pen, ink and pastel on paper,
38 × 52.5 cm - 1887
Inv. D 356 V/1962 - F 1393

Vincent recorded this view of Boulevard de Clichy from Place Blanche, a few steps from the flat where he and Theo lived in Rue Lepic. The Boulevard figured prominently in the life of the Impressionists: it was there that Toulouse-Lautrec's Moulin Rouge and Vincent's Café du Tambourin were located, that Cormon had his atelier, and that Frank Boggs, John Russell, Georges Seurat and Paul Signac lived. Though Impressionists of the previous generation such as Degas and Renoir also resided there, Van Gogh associated the neighbourhood with the younger generation, whom he dubbed the 'Impressionnistes du Petit Boulevard'. In this animated cityscape the Dutch artist focused for the first time on Parisian street life, which Impressionists such as Monet and Pissarro had previously treated with verve. The view in both drawing and painting is virtually the same, even if it is more

Vincent van Gogh
Boulevard de Clichy, Paris
Canvas, 46.5 × 55 cm - 1887
Inv. S 94 V/1962 - F 292

concentrated in the painted version and seen at closer range.

The similarities between them notwithstanding, there are some striking differences as well. The sense of depth is much more pronounced in the drawing, for instance, thanks in particular to the figures in the foreground which do not recur in the painting.

The colours in the sheet are less distinct, and the predominance of blue tints accounts for the relative coolness of the light. Finally in the painting, the artist's impressionistic manner enabled him to achieve a sunnier, more even effect. The naked trees suggest that both date from February-March 1887.

Vincent van Gogh
View from Vincent's Room on Rue Lepic
Canvas, 46 × 38 cm - 1887
Inv. S 57 V/1962 - F 341

Vincent van Gogh
A Corner of Montmartre
Canvas, 34.5 × 64.5 cm - 1887
Inv. S 14 V/1962 - F 347

Vincent van Gogh
Vegetable Gardens and the Moulin de Blute-Fin
on Montmartre
Canvas, 44.8 × 81 cm - 1887
Inv. S 15 V/1962 - F 346

These three works from the spring of 1887 show how Van Gogh's palette became more colourful following his exposure to Impressionism, and how he was also influenced by the stippling of the Neo-impressionists. Remarkably enough, he would sometimes combine these styles in his own idiosyncratic fashion in the same painting.

In his depiction of the vegetable gardens Van Gogh pretended that Montmartre had retained its rural character. Yet the charming canvas with figures strolling past the windmills leaves no doubt that, with its superb view, Montmartre was in fact fast becoming a popular destination for Parisians looking to escape the city for a day.

Vincent van Gogh
Self-portrait
Pasteboard, 19 × 14 cm - 1887
Inv. S 155 V/1962 - F 267

Vincent van Gogh
Self-portrait with Straw Hat
Pasteboard, 19 × 14 cm - 1887
Inv. S 157 V/1962 - F 294

If we compare these self-portraits to the first ones Van Gogh painted in Paris, we can see how far his use of colour had evolved in the course of a year. The browns of Nuenen gave way to blues, reds, greens, yellows and pinks. The brushwork also became more distinctive.

That Vincent felt comfortable in the rather elegant clothes he is wearing in these small works – none of which measures more than 19 by 14 centimetres – seems rather unlikely. He may have meant to dress according to contemporary bourgeois taste in order to practice the sort of formal portraiture

Vincent van Gogh
Self-portrait with Grey Felt Hat
Pasteboard, 19 × 14 cm - 1887
Inv. S 156 V/1962 - F 296

with which he hoped to earn a living someday.

The portrait of the young woman shows just how far Van Gogh had got on the road to becoming a portraitist. On 28 February 1887 his brother wrote their mother in Holland that 'Vincent has painted some portraits that have turned out well, but he never charges anything for them'. Though *Woman by a Cradle* is usually dated somewhat later – to the spring of 1887 – Theo could possibly have had this portrait in mind. Vincent may have borrowed the motif from female colleagues such as Berthe Morisot and Mary Cassatt, whose pictures in this vein he must have known. As regards technique, the canvas lies somewhere between Impressionism and Neo-impressionism, not unlike Toulouse-Lautrec's *Young Woman at a Table (Poudre de riz)* in the Van Gogh Museum.

The woman who sat for this portrait was identified several years ago. She is Léonie-Rose Davy, a niece of the art dealer Pierre-Firmin Martin, who married the tradesman Charles-Nicolas Charbuy. 'Père' Martin, as he was called, was a colleague and friend of Theo van Gogh. He dealt in such Impressionists as Guillaumin, Pissarro and Sisley and also had several of Vincent's works in stock. Given the pictures hanging on the wall behind her, Léonie-Rose probably sat for the portrait in the flat of the art dealer at N° 29 Rue St-Georges, where she herself had been living since 1883. As Martin's only heir, the young woman carried on his business after he died in 1891.

Vincent van Gogh
Woman Sitting by a Cradle
Canvas, 61 × 45.5 cm - 1887
Inv. S 165 V/1962 - F 369

Vincent van Gogh
A Pair of Shoes
Pasteboard, 33 × 41 cm - 1887
Inv. S 127 V/1962 - F 331

Vincent van Gogh
Still Life with Pansies
Canvas, 46 × 55.5 cm - 1886
Inv. S 180 V/1962 - F 244

The motif of a woman at a table, be she of questionable character or not, had been popular with Impressionists ever since Degas painted his famous *Absinthe Drinker*. Manet and Toulouse-Lautrec each treated the theme several times. The woman smoking a cigarette with the remarkable headdress, whom Van Gogh showed sitting at this tambourine-shaped table, is the proprietress of Café du Tambourin on Boulevard de Clichy. Of Italian origins, her name was Agostina Segatori. She had modelled regularly for painters in the 1860s, including Corot and Gérôme. Though Vincent seems to have been more than a friend to Segatori, who has evidently aged somewhat in the meantime, we know very little about their relationship – until, that is, they fell out at the end of the summer of 1887. Bernard tells us that Van Gogh used to pay for his board with flowers 'that last forever' – still lifes, in other words – which were used to decorate the café. The fact that the Pansies rest on a tambourine-shaped table would seem to indicate that he painted them in her establishment. We know from his correspondence that Van Gogh had been irritated by cafés without pictures while he was still living in Antwerp, and planned to remedy the situation with portraits and still lifes. Perhaps he got 'La Segatori' to see eye to eye.

It was in the Café du Tambourin that Van Gogh organised an exhibition of Japanese prints which – he claimed – would profoundly influence his Parisian colleagues Bernard and Anquetin. The portrait of Segatori makes reference to this exhibition. Not only is a Japanese painting or print indicated in the right background, but also other elements, such as the parasol, point to Japan. The still life with a pair of shoes likewise dates from the first half of 1887. Though there were precedents – such as pictures by the Realists François Bonvin and Théodule Ribot – shoes are a theme that has always been associated with Van Gogh. Indeed the Dutch artist's very first oil painting featured a pair of wooden clogs. Many have interpreted the motif as a symbol of the suffering with which his life was fraught. According to the Parisian painter François Gauzi, who studied in Cormon's atelier together with Van Gogh, his comrades found his subject matter somewhat bizarre. Yet it could not really be called revolutionary: Thomas Couture was already painting worn-out footwear in 1865, as though it were part of the stock-in-trade of any self-respecting Realist.

In all their simplicity these three works are clearly distinguished from the early still lifes Van Gogh painted as colour studies in Paris. The lighter palette makes a far more modern impression, and the contrast between each of the objects and the pattern in the background shows how much the artist had learned from Japanese prints. In Arles, Vincent would take this decorative approach one step further, as seen for instance in the background of his portraits of the postman Roulin and his wife the 'Berceuse'.

The fact that the stripes in the background of the two illustrated pictures are vertical while they are horizontal in one of the artist's other still lifes suggests that they are not modelled on the wallpaper in Van Gogh's flat, but on a piece of loose paper or fabric he used as a backdrop. If the application of the paint is any indication, Vincent did not spend much time on the still life with lemons. Despite the speed at which he was working, he convincingly described the light reflecting on the glass carafe. At the same time he demonstrated his knowledge of colour theory in the contrasts between the complementary colours yellow and purple in the plate of lemons, and between the red and green in the fore- and background. He must have been pleased with the results: the still life is one of the few works he not only signed but also dated.

Vincent van Gogh
Flowerpot with Chives
Canvas, 31.5 × 22 cm - spring 1887
Inv. S 183 V/1962 - F 337

Vincent van Gogh
Lemons on a Plate
Canvas, 21 × 26.5 cm - spring 1887
Inv. S 193 V/1962 - F 338

Vincent van Gogh
Lemons on a Plate and a Carafe
Canvas, 46.5 × 38.5 cm - spring 1887
Inv. S 20 V/1962 - F 340

The unusual oval format of these two still lifes corresponds to the shape of the Japanese tea boxes on which they are painted. The basket of germinating crocuses would seem to be a celebration of spring. Van Gogh saw the germinative power of a flower bulb or a grain of wheat as an emblem of human love. This constitutes the thematic link between the basket of flowers painted on the lid of the one box and the three novels on that of the other. The novels were all written by Naturalist authors dear to the artist. They are *Braves gens* by Jean Richepin, *Au bonheur des dames* by Emile Zola and *La fille Elisa* by Edmond de Goncourt. All three are set in contemporary Paris and concern the positive role of women in romantic relationships. Though we have no way of knowing whether this theme had any bearing on the artist's own life at the time, he did confide in his sister that he was 'still constantly [having] the most impossible and implausible love affairs, which I generally come away from with only injury and embarrassment'. As a painterly motif, the books are said to derive from Paul Signac, who is known to have done a very similar still life; yet Van Gogh painted his *Still Life with Bible*, showing Zola's novel *La joie de vivre* in the foreground, even before he left Nuenen.

Vincent van Gogh
Three Novels
Panel, 31 × 48.5 cm - spring 1887
Inv. S 181 V/1962 - F 335

Vincent van Gogh
Basket of Sprouting Flower Bulbs
Panel, 31.5 × 48 cm - spring 1887
Inv. S 63 V/1962 - F 336

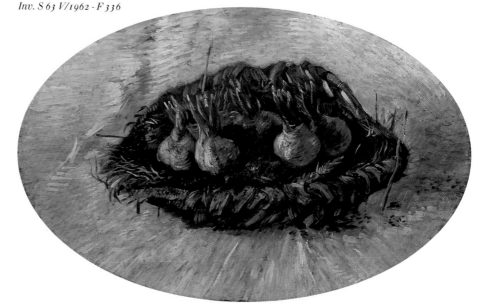

The still life with the stack of novels is actually a study for a slightly larger painting that was exhibited at the fourth exhibition of the Société des Artistes Indépendants in 1888. 'Romans parisiens' is also the subtitle of Richepin's *Braves gens*, one of the books seen in the oval still life. Though in contrast to that picture the titles of these books are illegible, they are likely to have been written by such Naturalists as Goncourt, Huysmans, Maupassant, Richepin and Zola, who depicted life 'as we feel it and thus satisfy our need to be told the truth [...] one can scarcely be said to belong to one's own time if one knows nothing about them'.

There has been a good deal of speculation about the date of this canvas. Given the confident touch, some specialists see it as a later variant from Arles. But a recent comparison between the two paintings showed that it was painted in Paris as a study for the definitive version, which was displayed at the Indépendants.

Vincent van Gogh
'Romans parisiens'
Canvas, 53 × 73.2 cm - 1887
Inv. S 21 V/1962 - F 358

Vincent van Gogh
The Ramparts of Paris with Horsetram and
Pedestrians (La Barrière)
Pencil, ink, pastel and watercolour,
39.5 × 53.5 cm - summer 1887
Inv. D 355 V/1962 - F 1400

In the summer of 1887 Van Gogh set out to paint a series of works depicting the fortifications around Paris. A number of his preparatory drawings of the fortifications survive, but to our knowledge he never got as far as transferring any of his ideas to canvas. One of the sketchbooks in the Van Gogh Museum contains several schematic studies of the ramparts. The two elaborately coloured drawings shown here were probably executed in the studio on the basis of them.
When Van Gogh was living in the capital Paris boasted over fifty city gates, constructed between 1841 and 1845. Their demolition commenced in the 1880s, after they had proven ineffective during the Franco-Prussian War of 1870-71. The present drawings show the fortifications around the Porte de Clichy, which the artist passed whenever he went to Asnières to paint. The tall building in the drawing on the right stood on Boulevard Bessières, just east of the Porte de Clichy.
An air of ill repute clung to the walls of Paris. They were flanked by poor neighbourhoods along much of their length, and became the scene of crime and prostitution after dark. In token of the 'terrains vagues' in which they

Vincent van Gogh
The Ramparts of Paris with Horsetram and
Pedestrians (La Barrière)
Pencil, ink and watercolour,
24 × 31.5 cm - summer 1887
Inv. D 420 V/1962 - F 1401

operated, the prostitutes themselves were known as 'terrières' or 'rempardeuses'. The writers Daudet and Huysmans and the illustrators Raffaëlli and Steinlen – all favourites of Van Gogh – had previously recorded the fortifications in word and image, and we may assume he was familiar with at least some of their efforts. The Van Gogh Museum preserves an anonymous engraving from the brothers' collection, moreover, entitled *Escaping Paris by Night*; it shows a group of men surreptitiously lowering themselves from the city walls by moonlight.

But the walls also had happier connotations for Parisians. On Sundays, they would seek out the fortifications to stroll or sit in the sun, as a respite from their daily existence in the dreary industrial zone of Clichy. Steinlen painted a radiant picture of the walls which, like Van Gogh's drawings, must date from around 1887 (Musée cantonal des Beaux-Arts, Lausanne); its palette and composition have much in common with the Dutch artist's handling of the motif.

In the river views Van Gogh created during the summer of 1887 he comes closest to the world of the Impressionists, with whose art he was well acquainted by now. The small view of the Seine, which he probably painted from the Ile des Ravageurs near Asnières, recalls the work of Monet and Sisley.

The influence of Pointillism is equally manifest in the work Van Gogh produced that summer. Indeed he frequently accompanied his friend Paul Signac, one of the style's pioneers, on excursions. Thematically this view of the Pont de la Grande-Jatte heralds that of the Pont de Trinquetaille, which Van Gogh would paint later in Arles.

Vincent van Gogh
The Seine with the Pont de la Grande-Jatte
Canvas, 32 × 40.5 cm - summer 1887
Inv. S 86 V/1962 - F 304

Vincent van Gogh
The Banks of the Seine
Canvas, 32 × 46 cm - summer 1887
Inv. S 77 V/1962 - F 293

Vincent van Gogh
Road along the Seine near Asnières
Canvas, 49 × 65.5 cm - summer 1887
Inv. S 55 V/1962 - F 299

Though there is nothing about the small
figure in this sunny river landscape that
would typify him as a painter, it is nonetheless tempting to identify him with
Vincent van Gogh. We know both from
contemporary descriptions and self-
portraits that a blue workman's smock
and a straw hat were his uniform during
this period.

Vincent van Gogh
Road in a Park at Asnières
Canvas, 33 × 42 cm - 1887
Inv. S 98 V/1963 - F 275

These two paintings of the Voyer d'Argenson park at Asnières show how Van Gogh employed rather divergent techniques in the same period, depending on the purpose of the work at hand. The view on the left is clearly a sketch, painted rapidly *en plein air* without figures.

Figures in a Park at Asnières represents Van Gogh's most ambitious but nonetheless idiosyncratic adaptation of the stippled manner developed by the Neo-impressionists. Rather than uniform dots of paint, he opted for a more expressive variation in the form of small, individual stripes or dashes in

different directions. This enabled him to emphasise the divergent textures of the ground, the shrubbery, the trees and the sky.

Thematically the picture bridges the worlds of Watteau's *fêtes galantes* and the sun-drenched gardens of Monet and Renoir. With this, one of his largest canvases, Van Gogh made his formal Parisian debut: in the winter of 1887-88 it hung alongside work by Seurat and Signac at the Théâtre Libre d'Antoine. Van Gogh's meagre Parisian correspondence makes no mention of the scene in the park, but in a letter from Arles he refers specifically to the

picture as 'the garden with the lovers'. As regards colour, one of his couples in a similar painting from Arles corresponds perfectly with the lovers seen here in Asnières: 'a couple in love, the man pale blue wearing a yellow hat, the upper part of the woman's body pink'.

With this theme Van Gogh upheld the tradition that began with Rubens's *Garden of Love* (Prado, Madrid), of which Watteau's *fêtes galantes* was another highpoint he admired. In the nineteenth century the *jardin d'amour* was revived by the painters Diaz and Monticelli. In a letter of February 1890 to the critic Albert Aurier, Vincent placed Monticelli on a par with Watteau as a painter of *fêtes galantes*, and as a character with Boccaccio. Van Gogh's description of Monticelli as a descendant of Boccaccio gives some idea of how the painter subconsiously viewed his own garden of love: 'A melancholic, rather resigned worrier who sees the festive world of entertainment, the lovers of his day, pass him by, and then paints and analyses them – he, the outcast'.

Vincent van Gogh
Vegetable Gardens on Montmartre
Canvas, 81 × 100 cm - April-June 1887
Inv. S 18 V/1962 - F 316

This view of Montmartre may have originally formed part of a series of landscapes full of 'cheerfulness and fresh air' which the artist considered suitable for decoration and which he mentioned in a letter to his brother in the summer of 1887, while Theo was visiting Holland. Be that as it may, Vincent regarded the large canvas worthy of admission to the Salon des Indépendants in 1888. Later on he thought about presenting it to the museum of modern art in The Hague by way of introducing himself to his countrymen as a full-fledged Impressionist. In response to a review of the Indépendants by Gustave Kahn, claiming that the artist had devoted too little attention to tonal values, Van Gogh argued that it was impossible to paint colour and tone at once: 'You can't be at the pole and at the equator simultaneously. You have to choose, as I hope to do. It will probably end up being colour'.

Five of these self-portraits were painted
on the backs of canvases Vincent had
previously used in Nuenen for studies:
heads of peasants, a composition sketch
for *The Potato Eaters* and still lifes. The
fact that he did not overpaint them
suggests that the studies continued to
be of some interest to him. They did,
after all, form part of a carefully
accumulated repertoire the artist
thought he might perhaps need at some
later date.

Most of these self-portraits have blue
backgrounds, were painted in the
summer of 1887 and are preoccupied
once again with colour and light.

As we can see, Vincent was still his own
principal model. Having just
successfully completed several more or

Vincent van Gogh
Self-portrait
Canvas, 41.5 × 31.5 cm
Inv. S 68 V/1962 - F 179v

Vincent van Gogh
Self-portrait
Canvas, 42 × 34 cm
Inv. S 97 V/1962 - F 269v

less Pointillist self-portraits, he now experimented with a broader, looser brushstroke and more thinly applied paint.

Compared with the series of small self-portraits he had made in the spring, his approach is now bolder, the result more psychologically charged. This time the painter seems to be as interested in representing different moods as in the technical aspects of his craft. Though they are artistically uneven, the growing self-analys evident in some of these works heralds the penetrating self-portraits of his final years.

Vincent van Gogh
Self-portrait
Canvas, 42 × 30 cm
Inv. S 163 V/1962 - F 524

In a letter to his former fellow student in Antwerp, Horace Mann Livens, Van Gogh wrote from Paris that he had done 'a dozen landscapes, frankly *green*, frankly *blue*'. Though he was probably not referring to these particular studies, they manifest the same determination to explore the infinite nuances of a particular colour. As a theme, forest views were pre-eminently suited to this end. The French term 'sousbois' denotes a closely observed woodland scene that emphasises the ground cover.

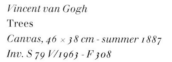

Vincent van Gogh
Trees
Canvas, 46.5 × 36 cm - summer 1887
Inv. S 78 V/1963 - F 307

Vincent van Gogh
Path in the Forest
Canvas, 46 × 38.5 cm - summer 1887
Inv. S 80 V/1962 - F 309

Vincent van Gogh
Trees
Canvas, 46 × 38 cm - summer 1887
Inv. S 79 V/1963 - F 308

Vincent van Gogh
Trees
Canvas, 46.5 × 55.5 cm - summer 1887
Inv. S 66 V/1962 - F 309a

Vincent could well have known the motif through the work of one of the Barbizon School painters, Diaz de la Peña, who specialised in the handling of light in forest views.

This closely related group of sylvan scenes from Vincent's Parisian period gave him ample opportunity to experiment with patterns of colour and light in a manner that recalls not only Diaz but also Monticelli and even Seurat. Pains were evidently taken to vary the texture of the paint, while at the same time a sense of depth is clearly suggested.

Ivy's propensity to cover trees and plants was something that always fascinated Van Gogh. Living in London in the mid-1870s he was charmed by the vine, and later, during his stay in Dordrecht in January 1877, he wrote of gazing out of his room 'on gardens with beech and poplar and so forth and the backs of houses [...] overgrown with ivy'. The sight reminded him of a favourite line from Charles Dickens: 'a strange old plant is the ivy green'. Toward the end of his life, while convalescing in the hospital of St-Rémy, Vincent again chose trees overgrown with ivy as the subject of several drawings and paintings.

Vincent van Gogh
Entrance to a Garden on Montmartre
Pencil, ink and watercolour, 31.6 × 24 cm -
summer 1887
Inv. D 148 V/1962 - F 1406

Vincent van Gogh
Barn on Montmartre, with Sunflowers
Pencil, ink and watercolour, 30.5 × 24 cm -
summer 1887
Inv. D 352 V/1962 - F 1411

These pages are filled with images of the summer of 1887: sunny views of Montmartre and the façade of an unidentified edifice. The potted shrubbery and the outdoor table have led some to think the building is a restaurant, but it could just as easily be the house of one of Vincent's painter friends, or perhaps the flat of the countess De la Boissière in Asnières, which according to one of the artist's letters was located above a restaurant. A year later, Vincent's own yellow house in Arles was painted the same colours as the exterior in the illustrated canvas. As he wrote his sister Wil in September 1888, 'The outside of my house here is painted the colour of fresh butter, with bright green shutters, and it gets direct sunlight'.

The coloured drawings represent picturesque corners of what was at that time the still somewhat rustic Butte Montmartre, with its panoramic prospects of Paris. Like the aforementioned picture of the 'restaurant', there is something unmistakeably Japanese about the drawings, which call to mind the artist's passion for Japanese woodcuts.One striking detail is the red, white and blue flag. At first glance it appears to be the French Tricolour, yet on closer inspection the stripes appear to be horizontal, not vertical, making the flag Dutch, not French. Could this be Van Gogh's idea of joke?

In the drawing of a barn with a vegetable garden at the edge of the Butte Montmartre, sunflowers make their first appearance in this volume. They would become the artist's universally recognised trademark.

Vincent van Gogh
Exterior of a Restaurant
Canvas, 18.5 × 27 cm - summer 1887
Inv. S 134 V/1962 - F 321

Vincent van Gogh
Sunflowers
Canvas, 21 × 27 cm - summer 1887
Inv. S 121 V/1963 - F 377

Vincent painted his first sunflowers in 1886, in a still life with other blooms (Kunsthalle Mannheim). They also occur in several painted and drawn Montmartre landscapes of 1887. The illustrated still life is a study preparatory to three ambitious pictures. Two of these were exhibited in the Restaurant du Chalet in late 1887, and subsequently exchanged with Gauguin for other works.

Vincent van Gogh
Wheatfield with Lark
Canvas, 54 × 65.5 cm - summer 1887
Inv. S 197 V/1962 - F 310

Amid the bustle of Paris, which by his own account eventually exhausted him, in the summer of 1887 Van Gogh found occasion to don a straw hat and paint *en plein air*. The straightforward design of the *Wheatfield with Lark* suits the simplicity of the theme. Only the bird, rising out of the windswept wheat, breaches the strict symmetry of the parallel strips of earth, wheat and sky. Thanks to the rich variation between the brushwork in each zone, the canvas seems to quiver with life. In the 1870s Van Gogh was already fond of Michelet's poem 'L'Alouette' (The Lark), and while he was still living in Antwerp, he wrote his brother about what the bird's song meant to him.

'Today, Sunday, it was almost spring. All I did this morning was walk about the entire city [...]. The weather was so beautiful that one could probably hear larks outside for the first time. In short, there was a bit of resurrection in the air'.

Vincent van Gogh
Self-portrait with Straw Hat
Pasteboard, 40.5 × 32.5 cm - summer 1887
Inv. S 164 V/1962

Toward the end of the time he spent in Paris Van Gogh painted several powerful still lifes with fruit. If one compares them with the studies of colour and tone from his Nuenen period, the progress he had made during the previous two years – under the influence of Impressionism – is clearly evident.

In the 1880s Seurat had begun dotting his frames with colours complementary to those in his pictures so as to enhance their effect. Apparently inspired by this, his Dutch colleague also experimented with frames. At times he painted a crimson line on the canvas itself. In the case of the still life dedicated to his brother, at first he applied red paint to the inner (or sight) edge of the frame – until, that is, he changed his mind, and finally painted the entire frame in tones consonant with the picture. The touches of paint on the framework occasionally resemble Japanese ideograms. They are also intended to approximate the crinkly effect of a type of Japanese print known as a 'crepon'. The Van Gogh Museum preserves a Chinese lacquer box containing a number of multi-coloured balls of wool. The artist used these to gauge the effect that various colour combinations would have. One of them perfectly matches the palette of the illustrated still life dedicated to Theo. It is a study not so much of colour contrasts as of closely related tones, in which various shades of yellow and brown are harmonised. Only here and there have a few dots of contrasting colours been applied.

Vincent van Gogh
Red Cabbages and Onions
Canvas, 50 × 64.5 cm - autumn 1887
Inv. S 82 V/1963 - F 374

Vincent van Gogh
White Grapes, Apples, Pears and Lemons
Dedicated 'à mon frère Theo'
Canvas, 48.5 × 65 cm - autumn 1887
Inv. S 23 V/1970 - F 383

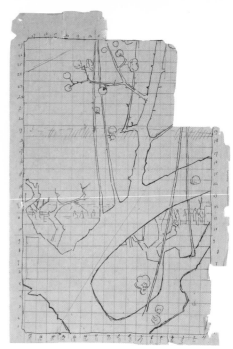

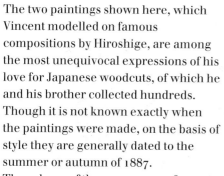

The two paintings shown here, which Vincent modelled on famous compositions by Hiroshige, are among the most unequivocal expressions of his love for Japanese woodcuts, of which he and his brother collected hundreds. Though it is not known exactly when the paintings were made, on the basis of style they are generally dated to the summer or autumn of 1887.

The colours of the canvases are far more intense than those of the original prints. After moving to Arles, where he thought he had found the perfect equivalent of Japan, Van Gogh claimed he no longer needed Japanese prints. It was enough 'to keep my eyes open and paint whatever strikes me in my immediate surroundings'. To what extent he had internalised Japanese graphic art can be inferred from the painting he made of an *Orchard in Blossom, Arles in the*

Background in April 1899: the trunks of the trees are rendered in lavender tints and outlined in black, just like those in the artist's painted copy after Hiroshige's plum.

The Van Gogh Museum preserves over 400 Japanese prints from the brothers' collection, many of them purchased from the noted dealer Siegfried Bing. Aside from the prints that inspired these pictures, Vincent's tracing of Hiroshige's plum also survives, which he made to facilitate the transition from print to painting.

The artist mounted both canvases in frames he himself painted with bright colours and decorated with calligraphic characters based on Japanese prints.

Vincent van Gogh
Japonaiserie: The Bridge in the Rain (after Hiroshige)
Canvas, 73 × 54 cm - summer/autumn 1887
Inv. S 114 V/1962 - F 372

Vincent van Gogh
Japonaiserie: The Courtesan (after Kesaï Eisen)
Canvas, 105.5 × 60.5 cm - summer/autumn 1887
Inv. S 116 V/1962 - F 373

On stylistic grounds the two canvases with skulls can be dated to the end of Vincent's Parisian period, but nothing is known about their original intention. They recall the drawings of skeletons he made in Antwerp, as well as the rather macabre picture of another smoking a cigarette. Though the skulls have been linked to the last self-portrait the artist painted in Paris, which contains references to death, it seems unlikely that the two works are more than studies, especially since they are devoid of props.

Vincent van Gogh
A Skull
Canvas, 43 × 31 cm - winter 1887/1888
Inv. S 123 V/1962 - F 297

Vincent van Gogh
A Skull
Canvas, 41.5 × 31.5 cm - winter 1887/1888
Inv. S 128 V/1962 - F 297a

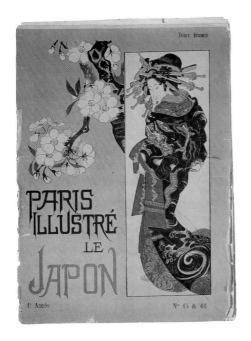

Cover of Paris Illustré: le Japon
May 1886

Van Gogh painted three Japonaiseries after Japanese prints. Though some have assumed they originally formed a single decoration, this seems unlikely given their divergent formats. The illustrated canvas is the largest of the three, and can be traced to a print by the Japanese artist Eisen. The print appeared on the cover of the May 1886 issue of the magazine *Paris Illustré* which was devoted to Japan. The same figure also occurs in the background of Van Gogh's portrait of the paint dealer Père Tanguy (Musée Rodin, Paris). Van Gogh himself fashioned an elaborate frame for the courtesan. It is decorated with cranes and frogs, both derogatory terms for prostitutes in French. The motif of the pond with water lilies and bamboo stalks seems to have been inspired by Hokusai, while the fat frog was modelled on a print by Utagawa Yoshimaru (1844-1907).

Vincent van Gogh
Self-portrait with Felt Hat
Canvas, 44 × 37.5 cm - winter 1887/1888
Inv. S 16 V/1962 - F 344

[I was] really broken, seriously ill and virtually an alcoholic'. The ambitious self-portrait of himself painting evokes his somber mood clearly. Dated 1888, the canvas is one of the last works Vincent painted before leaving for Arles. His description of the work in a letter to his sister Wil confirms the intense despondency he was feeling. 'A pinkish-grey countenance with green eyes, ashen hair, wrinkles in the forehead and around the mouth, stiff and wooden, a very red beard, rather untidy and sad, but the lips are full, a blue smock of rough linen and a palette with lemon-yellow, vermilion, Veronesque-green, cobalt-blue, in short, every colour except the orange beard on the palette, the only whole colours, however. The figure against a greyish-white wall.

'You'll say it looks a bit like the face of death in the book [*De kleine Johannes*, 1887] by [the Dutch author Frederik] van Eeden or something of the kind, good, but in the end, isn't such a figure – and it's not easy to paint oneself – in any case *something other* than a photograph? And you see, to my way of thinking Impressionism has this advantage over the rest, it's not trivial, and it seeks a deeper likeness than the photographer's'. The composition of the canvas has been compared to Cézanne's self-portrait at the easel. But in a letter to Emile Bernard of August 1888, Van Gogh himself referred to a self-portrait in the Louvre with a 'toothless laugh' by 'that old lion Rembrandt, a linen cloth on his head, palette in hand'.

The colour theory and stippled technique of the Neo-impressionists, with which Van Gogh became so well acquainted during his years in Paris, influenced his art in various ways. We have already seen how he employed the *pointille* in portraits and views of the capital, often to decorative ends. In this *Self-portrait with Felt Hat* of late 1887 or early 1888, he created a sort of aureole around himself using short lines or dashes. This personal variant of the Neo-impressionists' technique enabled him to determine the dynamic of a picture by simply varying the direction of his brushstrokes. In his eyes it was 'a real discovery'.

During his last months in Paris Van Gogh was deeply depressed. As he wrote Gauguin, 'When I left Paris

Vincent van Gogh
Self-portrait as Painter
Canvas, 65.5 × 50.5 cm - January 1888
Inv. S 22 V/1962 - F 522

Vincent van Gogh
View of a Butcher's Shop
Canvas, 39.5 × 32.5 cm - February 1888
Inv. S 119 V/1962 - F 389

Van Gogh in Arles

In February Van Gogh decided to leave Paris just as abruptly as he had come. He was drawn irresistably by the light of the south, and by the hope of finding something like Japan, the country that had captured his imagination in prints and novels. He also dreamed of organising an atelier for artists in the south – a dream that, with Gauguin's arrival in October 1888, seemed to have been realised. For reasons that have never become completely clear, he settled on the town of Arles. In one of his first letters to his brother from Provence he summarised what he had painted since making the move: 'an old Arlésienne, a landscape with snow, a view of a bit of pavement with a butcher's shop. The women here are very beautiful, that's absolutely true, unlike the museum in Arles, which is worthless [...]'.

This old woman was decidedly not one of the 'beautiful' Arlésiennes. The canvas recalls Emile Bernard's portrait of his grandmother, which Van Gogh had acquired from his friend in exchange for another work. As in that composition, a bed is summarily indicated in the background. *Old Woman from Arles*

harks back to the peasant types Vincent painted in Nuenen and then in Antwerp, under the influence of the 'tronies', or heads, of Frans Hals. But whereas Daumier and Gavarni had formed an important reference point when he painted his 'Heads of the People' in Nuenen, the expressive outlines of the old Arlésienne are patently inspired by Japanese prints, especially the actors' portraits in the brothers' collection.

Van Gogh's aspiration to become a figure painter and portraitist was finally realised in Arles. The important series of Zouave portraits, the postman Roulin, the peasant Patience Escalier and the 'Berceuse' all date from this period. Not until November 1888 did he paint a truly 'beautiful' Arlésienne, when he portrayed his friend Madame Ginoux in yellow and black.

Vincent van Gogh
Old Woman from Arles
Canvas, 58 × 42.5 cm -
February 1888
Inv. S 145 V/1962 -
F 390

These two small pictures, painted shortly after the artist's arrival in Arles, document the first signs of spring 1888. Van Gogh made another version of the almond sprig for his sister in early March. The charming canvas with a blossoming pear tree was conceived as the centrepiece of a tripartite decoration for the artist's brother. It has much in common with a Japanese print, including the vertical format and the marked angularity of the young tree. The division of the background into clearly demarcated areas and the blue sky partitioned by trees likewise call Japanese woodcuts to mind. Yet when Theo wanted to exhibit the work at Boussod & Valadon's, Vincent objected; the canvas was 'all too innocent' for that.

Vincent van Gogh
The Langlois Bridge
Canvas, 59.5 × 74 cm - March 1888
Inv. S 27 V/1962 - F 400

The draw bridge shown here, called the Pont de Réginelle (or Réginal), was known locally as the 'Pont de Langlois', after the bridge-keeper. It is located south of Arles, where it spans a canal running from that city to Port-de-Bouc. At the far left can be seen the lock through which the canal empties into the Rhône. Van Gogh's objective was to amalgamate the Dutch character of the landscape, the light of the south, and the shapes sharply silhouetted against the sky which he associated with Japan.

He painted several versions of the composition in March 1888, in both oil and watercolour. The variant in the Van Gogh Museum is the last and simplest of all. The figures in the fore- and middle ground have been suppressed, and the bridge is seen at a greater distance, so as to stress the length of the canal and thus to accentuate the similarity of the landscape to that of the artist's native Holland. In May 1888 he would return to the theme of the drawbridge once again.

In the nineteenth century, painters frequently employed flowering fruit trees as symbols of spring. Van Gogh was certainly familiar with works by Daubigny and Millet in which such symbolism occurred. In a period of less than a month, between 24 March and 21 April 1888, Vincent produced a total of fourteen canvases describing blossoming fruit trees in Arles. He hoped these 'motifs everyone enjoys' would sell well and possibly also convince his countrymen that he was making progress. It was only after he had picked up his brush that the idea occurred to him of grouping the canvases into decorative triptychs. In a letter to his brother of about 13 April 1888 he summarised what he had in mind. 'I'd really like to make that set of nine canvases. You see, we can consider this year's nine canvases as an initial design for a much larger, definitive

Vincent van Gogh
Blossoming Peachtrees
Canvas, 80.5 × 59.5 cm - April 1888
Inv. S 25 V/1962 - F 404

Vincent van Gogh
Sketch of the orchard triptych
from a letter to Theo of ca. 13 April 1888

Vincent van Gogh
The Pink Orchard
Canvas, 64.5 × 80.5 cm - March/April 1888
Inv. S 26 V/1962 - F 555

---

decoration to be carried out at about the same time next year using exactly the same motifs'.

Apparently forgetting his hopes of selling the orchards for the time being, on 9 April he wrote his colleague Bernard that in painting the series he had followed 'no system of brushwork whatsoever':

'Thick layers of paint, bits of canvas with no paint, here and there completely unfinished areas, overpainted areas, rough areas – in short, I think the result is disturbing, and sufficiently shocking to scare off people with preconceived notions about technique'.

Judging from another letter to Bernard which he wrote on about 21 April 1888, Vincent's intention was to create an ensemble with a great variety of colour: 'I have a stack of nine orchards: a white one, a pink one, a pink one verging on red, a blueish-white one, a greyish-pink one and a green one with pink'. Yet he was constantly plagued by fears that the canvases did not measure up, that they were somehow unworthy of the term 'tableau'. He was quite taken with his *White Orchard*, however, and stipulated the sort of frame it should have: 'white, cold and hard'. Indeed in a letter to his brother of February 1889, he suggested submitting that very canvas to the Indépendants for their next exhibition. The Van Gogh Museum is proud to be the sole proprietor of three orchard paintings conceived by the artist as an ensemble and – unlike the others – never separated. The central canvas, *Blossoming Peachtrees*, is the second version of this motif. Vincent dedicated the first, which is now in the Rijksmuseum Kröller-Müller at Otterlo, to the memory of his recently deceased cousin Anton Mauve. After learning of Mauve's death, Vincent suggested that Theo send his widow a picture – 'something tender and very cheerful', he thought. The flowering trees were just what he had in mind.

How far Van Gogh had distanced himself from the grey palette of his former teacher in the meantime! As he wrote his sister in late March 1888, 'You will understand that it's not possible to paint the southern landscape using Mauve's palette, for instance. He belongs to the north and is, and will remain, a master of the grey. Nowadays the palette is very colourful, sky blue, orange, pink, vermilion, bright yellow, bright green, bright wine-red, violet. But by intensifying *all* the colours one comes back to peace and harmony. Something occurs in nature similar to what happens in Wagner's music, which, though played by a large orchestra, is nonetheless intimate'. Vincent would certainly have painted more orchards that spring, had it not been for the weather. 'The wind makes it very difficult for me to paint, but I secure my easel by driving stakes into the ground and then work regardless. It's too beautiful'.

To keep his brother abreast of his progress he sent coloured drawings of the pictures to Paris, taking care to point out that 'Of course the colours in the painted studies are brighter'. The illustrated watercolour with flowering peachtrees formed part of just such a shipment. Because certain pigments have faded somewhat in the meantime, the contrast between the paintings and the watercolour sketch is no longer as pronounced as it once was. In fact, because the canvases have faded the watercolour [see following page] probably gives a better idea of how colourful they were when they were freshly painted than do the canvases themselves.

Vincent van Gogh
The White Orchard
Canvas, 60 × 81 cm - April 1888
Inv. S 24 V/1962 - F 403

Vincent van Gogh
Blossoming Peachtrees
Black chalk and watercolour on paper,
45.5 × 30.5 cm - March 1888
Inv. D 208 V/1962 - F 1469

Vincent van Gogh
View of Arles with Irises in the Foreground
Canvas, 54 × 65 cm - May 1888
Inv. S 37 V/1962 - F 409

On 12 May 1888 Vincent wrote Theo about a landscape study he had just finished, a 'meadow full of bright yellow buttercups, a ditch with irises, green leaves and purple flowers, the town in the background, some grey willows, and a strip of blue sky. If the meadow doesn't get mowed, I'd like to do this study again, as the subject was very beautiful and I had some trouble getting the composition. A little town surrounded by fields all covered with yellow and purple flowers; exactly – can't you see it? – like a Japanese dream'. A week later he described the canvas to Bernard in virtually the same terms: 'That sea of yellow with a band of violet irises, and in the background that coquettish little town with its pretty women!'

Vincent van Gogh
The Sea at Les Saintes-Maries-de-la-Mer
Canvas, 51 × 64 cm - June 1888
Inv. S 117 V/1962 - F 415

One of the things that appealed to Van Gogh about living in Arles was the proximity of the Mediterranean. Yet it was not until late May that he actually visited the coast. At first he considered Marseilles, but finally settled on the picturesque fishing village of Les Saintes-Maries-de-la-Mer, where in the space of a few short days – from 30 May until 3 June – he produced no less than two seascapes, a village view and nine drawings.

Since his Scheveningen seascape of 1882, Vincent had painted no more 'marines'. Three sea and beach views constituted the fruits of his Mediterranean excursion. Two of these works are now in the Van Gogh Museum. Painted with speed and vigour, the illustrated seascape has all the marking of a picture painted *en plein air*. The bold red signature suggests the artist was satisfied with the results, and at the same time provides 'a red accent in the green'.

The canvas corresponds to Van Gogh's enthusiastic description of the sea: 'like the colour of mackerels, in other words changing – you don't always know if it's green or purple, you don't always know if it's blue, since before you know it the constantly shifting reflection has taken on a pink or a grey tint'.

Vincent van Gogh
Fishing Boats on the Beach at Les Saintes-
Maries-de-la-Mer
Canvas, 65 × 81.5 cm - June 1888
Inv. S 28 V/1962 - F 413

The view of the boats on the beach was done in the studio, based on a drawing made on the spot. As Vincent explained to Theo: 'When I went out very early in the morning, I made the drawing of the boats and am now making a painting of it, a size 30 canvas with more sea and sky on the right. That was before the boats departed in great haste, which I'd watched them do every morning but, since they leave so early, had no time to paint'.

Understandably the work, which is actually a bit smaller than Van Gogh told his brother, has been dubbed a 'still life with four boats'. The artist himself described the scene to Emile Bernard as 'small green, red and blue boats, so beautiful in form and colour that they remind one of flowers'. The stylised handling of the vessels betrays once more the influence of Japan. Van Gogh planned to make a second journey to Les Saintes-Maries but never returned. On 12 June he wrote his brother 'I haven't been back to Saintes-Maries; they've finished painting the house and I had to pay [...]'.

After the series of orchards and the never fully realised series of seascapes, Van Gogh focused his attention on peasant life during the summer of 1888. His first step in this direction was a series of wheatfields. The smaller of the two canvases shown here was probably painted within a matter of hours and has the character of an (albeit brilliant) sketch.

Around 12 June Vincent wrote Theo that he was working on a large, ambitious picture 'in the genre of the two landscapes of the Butte Montmartre', only 'stronger' and with 'slightly more style'. *The Harvest* shows the plain of La Crau outside Arles. In this panoramic landscape, painted from a lofty vantage point, it takes some effort to find the human activity that the title leads one to expect. At the left the composition is framed by the ruins of the fortified monastery of Montmajour and the Alpilles range.

As the orchards were an emblem of spring, so *The Harvest* symbolised summer. Van Gogh clearly found the Provençal landscape no less exciting once it 'began to get parched. There's old gold, bronze and copper in everything, and with the azure-green of the incandescent sky that gives a delicious, extraordinarily harmonious colour, with broken tints as with Delacroix'.

Van Gogh carefully prepared the work with detailed pen drawings. The canvas itself he painted 'in a single lengthy sitting', though he retouched it later.

Vincent van Gogh
Wheatfield
Canvas, 54 × 65 cm - June 1888
Inv. S 146 V/1962 - F 411

Vincent van Gogh
The Harvest
Canvas, 73 × 92 cm - June 1888
Inv. S 30 V/1962 - F 412

At an art gallery in Paris the Dutchman had seen a canvas with a similar harvest by Cézanne. Recalling that picture and comparing it to his own *Harvest*, he concluded that the French master had captured 'the hard side of Provence', and that there were therefore few essential parallels between the two works. 'I only want to say that Cézanne, like Zola, grew up in the countryside. He therefore knows it so well that in your head you have to make the same consideration to arrive at comparable tones. Obviously the two pictures could stand being juxtaposed, but they would have nothing in common'. Van Gogh felt more affinity with the landscapes of his fellow country-men, the seventeenth-century Dutch master Philips Koninck, who excelled at panoramas, than with Cézanne's.

For all Van Gogh's modesty, he was well aware that his depiction of the harvest on the plain of La Crau was in fact a masterpiece. To Theo he wrote not once but three times that 'The [...] canvas knocks absolutely all the others dead'.

From 20 until 23 June 1888 it did nothing but pour with rain in Arles. It was all the same to Vincent: 'I finally have a model – a Zouave – a bull-necked youth with a small face and the look of a tiger. I started out with one portrait and then did another. The half-length I painted of him was terribly garish – in a uniform the colour of blue enamelled saucepans, with faded reddish-orange passementerie and two lemon-yellow stars on the chest, an ordinary blue and very hard to do. I placed his feline, bronzed head with red hat against a green door and an orange brick wall. So it's a crude combination of colours that don't match, not easy to manage. The studies I made of it seem very harsh, but then I'd like to work on vulgar, even loud portraits like this all the time. I learn from it, which is what I most want from my work'.

In a similar vein Van Gogh described the work to his friend Emile Bernard, to whom he dedicated a watercolour drawing of the portrait: 'It is harsh and utterly ugly and badly done. Yet because I tackled genuine difficulties in it, it could clear the path for the future. The figures I make are almost always detestable in my own eyes and the more so in those of others; yet it's from studying the figure that you can learn the most'.

Vincent van Gogh
The Ploughed Field
Canvas, 72.5 × 92.5 cm - September 1888
Inv. S 40 V/1962 - F 574

During the summer of 1888 Van Gogh produced a great many landscapes. He considered the illustrated canvas one of the most successful, though the motif was 'nothing but clods of earth, the furrows in the colour of old wooden shoes under a forget-me-not blue sky with white flakes'. In his eyes this landscape was 'more peaceful' than the others. 'If the work always went so smoothly', he sighed in a letter to his brother, 'I would worry less about making money, for people would be drawn to it more readily if the technique were more harmonious'. Because of the heavily applied paint – 'the present studies are really made from a single *stream of paint*' – he realised the canvas would dry slowly. 'You have to treat pictures with thick impastos like strong wine: they have to rest'.

189   ARLES

Vincent van Gogh
Vase with Sunflowers
Canvas, 95 × 73 cm - January 1￼
Inv. S 31 V/1962 - F 458

In May 1888 Van Gogh rented 'the yellow house' on Place Lamartine, not far from the Rhône. He used the summer to put a fresh coat of paint on the building, where he already had his studio. It was there that the Zouave sat for him. For the interior the artist designed an ambitious decorative scheme in preparation for the arrival of Gauguin, the point being to make the house a 'refuge atelier' and a 'vrai maison d'artiste'. Knowing how much Gauguin liked the sunflower still lifes he had painted in Paris, in late August Vincent designed a decoration for his friend's room comprising no less than twelve of them, which he planned to frame in 'thin slats, painted in orange minium'. He threw himself into the project 'with the enthusiasm of someone from Marseilles eating bouillabaisse', but ultimately decided only two were worthy of his friend. But then they were – in Gauguin's words – 'a perfect example of a style that is completely Vincent'.

The *Vase with Sunflowers* in the Van Gogh Museum is actually a replica of one of the two pictures for Gauguin, painted by Van Gogh in January 1889. In February 1890 Vincent wrote the critic Albert Aurier that he saw the sunflowers as a symbol of 'gratitude'. In late September 1888 Van Gogh sent his brother a sketch of the picture he had just made of the Yellow House 'beneath a sulfur-yellow sun, beneath a sky of pure cobalt. [...] It's powerful, those yellow houses in the sun and then the incomparable brilliance of the blue. [...]

The pink house with green shutters on the left, standing in the shade of a tree, is the restaurant where I go to eat every day. My friend the postman lives at the end of the street on the left, between the two railroad bridges'.

Van Gogh called the canvas *The Street (La rue)*. Johannes Vermeer's *The Little Street* in Amsterdam's Rijksmuseum presumably suggested the title to him.

Vincent van Gogh
The Street (The Yellow House)
Canvas, 72 × 91.5 cm - September 1888
Inv. S 40 V/1962 - F 464

On 16 October 1888 Van Gogh sent his brother a detailed description of the picture showing 'just my bedroom'. Having spent the entire summer painting feverishly outdoors, no wonder he was determined that the canvas evoke '*rest*', or '*sleep*'. The weary artist's sturdy furniture served to convey 'inviolable repose'. The austere interior of the yellow house reminded Vincent of the interiors painted by Johannes Bosboom, one of his favourite members of the Hague School, 'with the red tiles, the white walls, the pine or walnut furniture, the patches of vivid blue sky and the green seen through the windows'.

Shortly afterwards Van Gogh depicted a sturdy chair with rush seat like that at the left in *The Bedroom*. He placed it in the context of a symbolic self-portrait that took the form of a still life. He personified Gauguin in a similar fashion: as an armchair of a bit more elegant design. Whereas his own chair is rendered realistically by daylight, Gauguin's 'portrait' is a nocturne. The two modern novels and burning candle stand for his colleague's art, which relied more heavily on the imagination than his own.

Vincent van Gogh
Gauguin's Chair
Canvas, 90.5 × 72.5 cm - November 1888
Inv. S 48 V/1962 - F 499

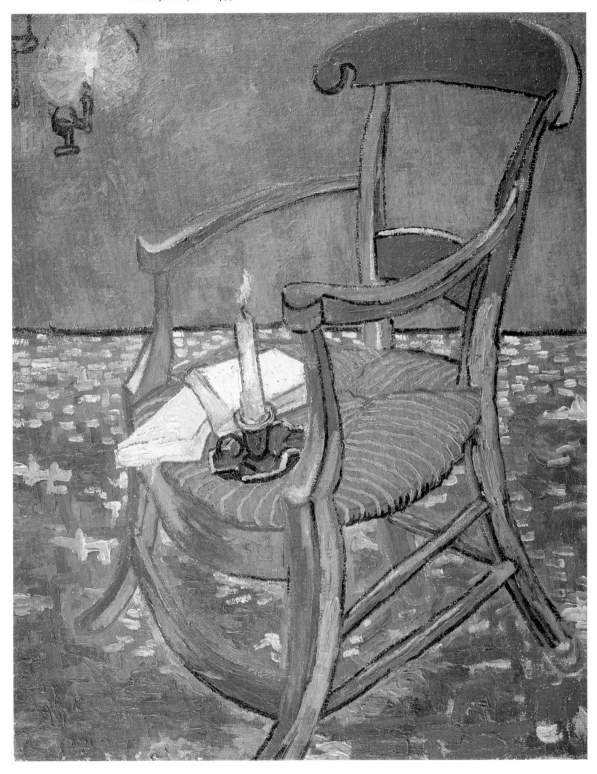

Before going to Arles, Gauguin had spent some time working in Brittany. Paris was expensive for painters, and the constant exposure to new ideas could sometimes bewilder an impressionable artistic temperament. Hence the Frenchman's departure for the coast in early February 1888. The Bretons had long attracted painters of country life, who were intrigued by their picturesque traditions and costumes. Descended from Celts and living in isolation on their peninsula, the Bretons were considered pre-eminently 'primitive' and unspoilt, which explains their fascination for urban artists.

Intent on 'drinking in the character of the populace and the landscape', Gauguin moved into the pension Gloanec in Pont-Aven. In June 1888 he painted *La Ronde des petites Bretonnes*, showing girls dancing prettily while the hay was being made, a reprise of a theme he had previously treated in 1886. While a painted version of the composition shows the girls full length against a view of Pont-Aven, the illustrated pastel observes them at close range against a clear blue sky. The undulating outline follows the girls' movements as they dance.

In its present form the drawing was probably retouched after serving its original purpose as a study preparatory to the large painted versions of the same motif. Gauguin presented it to Theo van Gogh as a gift, out of gratitude for the 50 francs the dealer had sent him in Brittany.

The theme of dancing Breton girls subsequently became popular with members of the group of artists known as the Nabis, which included Maurice Denis, Paul Sérusier and Georges Lacombe.

Paul Gauguin
Paris 1848-1903 Atuana
Study of Breton Girls Dancing ('Ronde Breton')
Charcoal, pastel and watercolour, 24 × 41 cm -
1888
Inv. D 663 V/1963

Emile Bernard
Lille 1868-1941 Paris
Road in Brittany with Figures
Watercolour, 30.7 × 20.2 cm - July 1888
Inv. D 646 V/1962

Emile Bernard
Breton Woman in an Orchard
Watercolour, 32 × 19.1 cm - July 1888
Inv. D 645 V/1962

Though Emile Bernard had already been introduced to Gauguin in 1886 and the two artists had met again at the end of that summer in Brittany, it was only later that they began collaborating. It all started in July 1888, when Van Gogh wrote Bernard that Gauguin was in Pont-Aven. The two artists' subsequent meeting marked the beginning of a period of reciprocal influence. Around 23 July, Van Gogh thanked Bernard for sending him two colourful drawings of Breton women. 'I find the plane-tree road along the sea with two women talking in the foreground and figures walking very beautiful. Also the woman under the apple tree [...]'. Both sheets are executed in the Cloisonnist manner characteristic of the school of Pont-Aven. Their decorative – and occasionally also caricatural – conception anticipates the series of *Bretonnerie* prints Bernard would create in late 1888/early 1889. When, in late October 1888, Gauguin joined Van Gogh in Arles, he had with him a painting with Breton women by Bernard; Vincent was no less enthusiastic about that work, with its 'beautiful composition and – in all its naïveté – distinguished palette'.

Emile Bernard
Self-portrait with Portrait of Gauguin
Canvas, 46.5 × 55.5 cm - September 1888
Inv. S 206 V/1962

Van Gogh received these self-portraits – both painted in Pont-Aven in September 1888, where Bernard and Gauguin were living at the time – in Arles in early October. They were intended as expressions of friendship, albeit elicited by Vincent himself: having read that Japanese artists exchanged their work he had invited his friends to do the same. But rather than portraying one another as he had suggested – Bernard apparently shrank from the thought of painting his distinguished confrère, Gauguin – the two opted for self-portraits instead. Possibly as a concession to their Dutch colleague, they included each other's likenesses in the background. And in

the lower left corner of his canvas Bernard painted a Japanese print, an allusion to the art form he had come to know through his friend.

Van Gogh preferred Bernard's self-portrait – 'a few simple tones, a few dark lines, but [...] as elegant as a real, true Manet' – to Gauguin's, which emanated such melancholy as to alarm him. The older artist had cast himself as Jean Valjean, the protagonist of Victor Hugo's novel *Les Misérables*, because like Valjean, he fancied himself a social outcast, and like Hugo's hero, he took revenge 'by doing good'. By the same token, his features evoke Valjean's 'nobility and inner gentleness. The ruttish blood that floods the face and the fiery hues enveloping the eyes are the burning lava that makes our painter's soul seethe'. Gauguin called the background 'feminine' on account of the 'child-like flowers', which stood for artistic purity.

Paul Gauguin
Portrait of Joseph-Michel Ginoux
Canvas, 40 × 31 cm - 1888
Inv. S 256 V/1962

Vincent van Gogh?
Portrait of Gauguin?
Canvas, 37 × 33 cm
Inv. S 257 V/1962

Paul Gauguin
Study for 'Woman in the Hay'
Watercolour, 26.3 × 40.4 cm - 1888
Inv. D 682 V/1962

In the summer and autumn of 1888 Van Gogh painted countless portraits, especially members of the families Ginoux and Roulin. After reaching Arles on 25 October, Gauguin painted some of the same models, including Joseph-Michel Ginoux.

The identification of the figure seen at an angle from behind with Gauguin has been challenged, nor is the attribution of the canvas to Van Gogh universally accepted. On the other hand, it has been argued that hardly any other artist could be its author, the more so as we can be certain the canvas once belonged to Theo van Gogh.

The attitude of the figure is a credible approximation of a painter at work, and the German art historian Roland Dorn recognised the blurred outlines of Gauguin's *Woman in the Hay (Dans le foin)* in the background. In mid-November 1888 Vincent wrote his brother about that canvas, of which the Van Gogh Museum still preserves a watercolour study: 'Gauguin is working on a very original woman in the hay, with pigs. It promises to be very beautiful and to have great style'.

Van Gogh was painting sunflowers when Gauguin portrayed him in early December, placing one of his own landscapes in the background. The final result must have shocked Van Gogh, who supposedly exclaimed 'That's me, all right, but me as a madman'. In September 1889, Vincent confessed to his brother that he had been 'dead tired and extremely tense' when the portrait was painted.

Paul Gauguin
Van Gogh Painting Sunflowers
Canvas, 73 × 91 cm - November 1888
Inv. S 225 V/1962

Paul Gauguin
Paris 1848-1903 Atuana
Women on the Banks of the River, Tahiti
Canvas, 43.5 × 32.5 cm - 1892
Inv. S 222 V/1962

In December 1888 a 'huge catastrophe' occurred. There had been tension between Van Gogh and Gauguin while they were sharing the Yellow House in Arles. Exactly two months after the latter's arrival, on 23 December to be precise, the situation came to a dramatic head: Vincent threatened his friend with a knife. With characteristic self-control Gauguin just managed to escape. That same evening Vincent mutilated his ear and was promptly admitted to the local hospital; not until 7 January was he released. Gauguin left Arles immediately after the incident, putting an end to Van Gogh's dream of a 'southern atelier'.

After recovering from the crisis, at first Van Gogh was bitter about Gauguin's desertion. The two painters eventually made amends, however, and indeed Theo van Gogh remained Gauguin's dealer until his death in January 1891. In April 1891 Gauguin decided to leave Europe once again in search of an unspoilt society. This time he chose the South Pacific island of Tahiti, where in 1892 he painted this colourful landscape. About his initial hesitation to use strong colours Gauguin wrote in *Noa Noa*: 'the landscape, with its pure, intense colours astonished and blinded me [...]. Yet it was so simple to paint what I saw, to put a red or blue on my canvas without any premeditation! Golden shapes in the streams enchanted me: why did I hesitate, instead of letting all that gold and all that sunny joy flood my canvas?' In August 1893 Gauguin returned to Paris, bringing his first Tahitian adventure to an end.

Paul Gauguin
Paris in the Snow
Canvas, 71.5 × 88 cm - 1894
Inv. S 223 V/1962

Following the death of the Parisian art dealer Julien-François Tanguy in 1893, several Van Goghs owned by Gauguin found their way by mistake into the hands of Theo van Gogh's widow, who had been keeping some 200 of her brother-in-law's works with Tanguy. At Gauguin's request she promptly returned his property. Out of gratitude for her compliance the Frenchman sent her his *Paris in Winter*, along with his *Women by the River* of 1892.
Paris in the Snow is a surprisingly 'Impressionist' picture. It was painted in February 1894 in homage to the late painter Gustave Caillebotte, who had helped the fledgling artistic movement get on its feet. After lengthy public discussion his important collection had finally been accepted by the French State. In 1878 Caillebotte himself had painted a *View of Rooftops, Effect of Snow* (Musée d'Orsay, Paris), to which Gauguin's depiction of the view from his studio on Rue Vercingétorix seems to refer. Considering it is a snowscape, his canvas is remarkably colourful.

Vincent van Gogh
The Sower
Canvas, 32 × 40 cm - November 1888
Inv. S 29 V/1961 - F 451

In June 1888 Van Gogh sought to realise a dream he had long cherished: he painted his own version of Millet's *Sower*, which had fascinated him ever since he first picked up a brush. Yet the artist was not satisfied with the results, an ambitious amalgamation of things observed and imagined. He went on changing many of the details of the picture (now in the Rijksmuseum Kröller-Müller) till finally he concluded it was a 'flop': the large format notwithstanding, the Otterlo canvas was nothing more than a 'glorified study' in his eyes. In the course of 1888 he continued to produce several variants,

until in late November he made his last attempt to improve on his hero's masterpiece: 'another sower. Large lemon-yellow disc as sun. Yellow-green sky with pink clouds. The earth violet, the sower and the tree Prussian blue; size 30 canvas'. The smaller version of the composition in the Van Gogh Museum illustrated here is probably a study for the work, which is now in the Bührle Collection, Zurich. In reply to a favourable letter from his brother Vincent indicated that he, too, was satisfied with the results: 'Occasionally a canvas becomes a painting, like *The Sower*, which I, too,

think is better than the first'.
The placement of the figure's head against the sun lends the work a certain religious air. The prominent arrangement of the tree is usually traced to Gauguin's *Vision after the Sermon: Jacob Wrestling with the Angel* (Edinburgh, National Gallery), which features a similar diagonal, but the composition could just as easily have been inspired by a Japanese print.

'I've made portraits of *an entire family*', Vincent wrote Theo with evident satisfaction in early December 1888, 'the family of the postman [Roulin], whose head I've done before: husband, wife, baby, the small boy and the 16-year-old son, all types and really French, though they look like Russians. Size 15 canvases. [...] I hope to go on with this and to paint more serious poses and pay for them with portraits. And if I manage to make *that entire family* better still, then at least I'll have done something to my own liking'. Though the illustrated portraits are smaller than those the artist mentioned in his letter, which were painted in late November, not much time could have elapsed between the execution of the two groups.

Since Camille Roulin, 'the small boy' Vincent referred to in his letter, was born in July 1877, he would have been eleven when this portrait was painted. Another version of it hangs in the Philadelphia Museum of Art. Little Marcelle was born on 31 July 1888; three versions of her likeness are known.

Vincent sent the baby's portrait to Theo in Paris in May 1889. On 5 July Theo's wife Jo, who was expecting a child, wrote her brother-in-law that everyone admired the canvas. Indeed the couple was so pleased with the portrait that they hung it in such a way that 'from my place at table I have a perfect view of the child's big blue eyes, lovely little hands and round cheeks. I like to think that our baby will be just as strong, just as healthy and just as beautiful – and that one day his uncle will want to make a portrait of him!' Marcelle must indeed have had a healthy constitution, for she died only in 1980, at the age of 91!

Vincent van Gogh
Portrait of Marcelle Roulin
Canvas, 35 × 24.5 cm - December 1888
Inv. S 167 V/1962 - F 441

Vincent van Gogh
Portrait of Camille Roulin
Canvas, 40.5 × 32.5 cm - December 1888
Inv. S 166 V/1962 - F 538

Vincent van Gogh
Orchard in Bloom
Canvas, 72.5 × 92 cm - April 1889?
Inv. S 38 V/1962 - F 511

In the spring of 1889 Van Gogh resolved to take up his series of blossoming orchards once again, only to be delayed by his admission to the hospital following a subsequent breakdown. On 24 March 1889 he wrote his brother that he expected to be back at work before long, and by early April he was ready to begin. Around the tenth of the month he sent his friend Paul Signac a sketch of the orchard with the silhouette of Arles in the background. The picture itself – 'almost entirely green, with a bit of lilac and grey' – had been painted on a rainy day.

In mid-April Vincent wrote Theo that he had already finished six studies, 'including two large orchards. I'm in a great hurry, because those effects are so ephemeral'. By the time he wrote his sister at the end of the month, however, the artist was clearly disappointed: 'Last year I made ten or twelve orchards and this year I have only four, so the work isn't going very well'. When exactly the large illustrated orchard was painted is uncertain. Some have argued it was made the previous year, but the style has more in common with the orchards Vincent painted in the spring of 1889.

Vincent van Gogh
Orchard in Bloom with Arles in the Background
Canvas, 50.5 × 65 cm - April 1889
Inv. S 36 V/1962 - F 515

This closely observed bit of nature belongs to a series of studies of flowers and clumps of grass. Though difficult to date, the canvases were probably painted toward the end of Vincent's stay in Arles. In August 1888 he had made several studies of dusty thistles along the side of a road, all of the same format. The illustrated picture may be one of the 'spring studies' he wrote Theo about in April 1889.

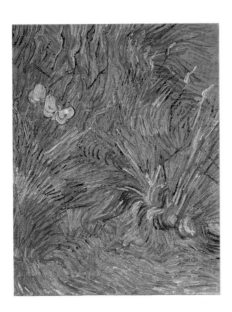

Vincent van Gogh
Garden with Flowers and Two White Butterflies
Canvas, 55 × 45.5 cm - spring 1889
Inv. S 110 V/1962 - F 402

Vincent van Gogh
Steps in the Garden of St Paul's Hospital in St-Rémy
Black chalk, pencil, ink and watercolour,
62 × 44.5 cm - May 1889
Inv. D 438 V/1962 - F 1535

Van Gogh in St-Rémy

On 8 May Van Gogh arrived by train at the mental hospital St-Paul-de-Mausole in St Rémy-de-Provence, which he and Theo had chosen. Dr Peyron, to whose care the artist had entrusted himself, inscribed the following diagnosis in his book of patients: 'Though at this moment he appears to have fully regained his senses, he feels he lacks the strength and courage to live independently, and has therefore asked to be admitted to this institution of his own accord. In light of his previous history I have come to the conclusion that Mr van Gogh suffers from epileptic fits, and that it would be advisable to keep him under observation here for a good while'. At the end of the first fortnight, Dr Peyron informed Theo that Vincent was doing well: 'He spends the whole day drawing in the garden'. The doctor had promised the artist that he could work outside the walls of the asylum as soon as his condition stabilised. Peyron confided to Theo, however, that his brother's chances of a lasting recovery were slim, 'since I have good reason to believe the attack he had is caused by a form of epilepsy. If this proves to be the case, we must fear the worst'. In mid-July Van Gogh's illness struck again, while he was painting in a field. It was not until late August that he regained his strength. At that point, while confined to his room, he started painting a series of copies after prints by Millet as well as a number of portraits. In late September he ventured forth from the institution again, this time to paint the surrounding hills and olive orchards and the main street of St-Rémy. But more attacks followed in December and January. Despite the constant assaults on his mental health, Vincent sent no less than seven shipments of pictures to Theo from St-Rémy. The 'bright yellow note' of Arles gave way to a more subdued palette, which the artist himself associated with a yearning for the north. Qualitatively the sojourn in St-Rémy signified anything but a decline. It was there that Van Gogh produced a magnificent series of olive orchards and cypresses, as well as views of the surrounding hills – such as *The Reaper* – and flower still lifes like *The Irises*.

Vincent van Gogh
Trees and Bushes in the Garden of St Paul's
Hospital at St-Rémy
Watercolour and gouache, 46.5 × 62 cm - May 1889
Inv. D 334 V/1962 - F 1533

Vincent van Gogh
Olive Grove
Canvas, 45.5 × 59.5 cm - June 1889
Inv. S 44 V/1962 - F 709

In the peaceful surroundings of St Paul's Hospital in St-Rémy, Van Gogh's fear of insanity gradually subsided. The confrontation with his fellow patients reconciled him with the fate of other artists who had had to struggle with their psyches, such as Matthijs Maris, Monticelli and Méryon. 'I see those artists regain their calm aura and can you imagine how much it means to rediscover old confrères?'

In the immediate proximity of the asylum there were several small olive groves. Starting in June, Vincent made some attractive studies of them, though as he wrote his brother he found the motif 'very difficult'. His goal was to capture the characteristic qualities of the olive trees in the hope that this quintessentially Provençal motif would become 'a personal impression [...] just as the sunflowers are for the yellow tints'. In a letter to Bernard he compared the silvery grey of the olive trees with that of Corot, but even the French master had not captured their essence: 'it has never been done before, whereas various artists have managed to paint apple trees and willows, for instance'. Vincent also drew inspiration from his fellow patients. The so-called 'one-eyed' man, assigned by some scholars to his Arles period, whom the artist portrayed in 1889, was certainly one of the inmates. No sooner did he receive it in May 1890 as part of a shipment of pictures from St-Rémy than Theo liked the canvas, which he dubbed the 'fellow with the puffy face'.

Vincent van Gogh
The Man with the Puffy
Face
Canvas, 56 × 36 cm -
1889
Inv. S 113 V/1962 - F 532

208

Since Van Gogh was not permitted to leave the hospital garden when he was first in St-Rémy, he had to content himself with whatever motifs he could find within its walls. Fortunately there were plenty of picturesque nooks from which to choose. The tall pines towered over the 'tall and untidy grass [...] mixed with all sorts of periwinkel', on which the sun shining through the trees created fascinating patterns of light and shade. In a letter to his brother of 6 July Vincent mentioned this size 30 canvas for the first time. It later became a favourite of Jo van Gogh, who loved 'the delicious coolness and freshness of the *sousbois*. I feel like I know that spot and have been there often – I love it so much'. Indeed her affection for the picture was so great that the family held on to it.

In mid-July 1889 Van Gogh was felled by another serious attack in St-Rémy. Not until 22 August was he able to write again, at which point he informed his brother that the illness had overcome him near the entrance to a quarry 'while I was painting in the field on a windy day'. Despite the attack he managed to finish the canvas. The colours were gloomy: 'dull and subdued, broken green, red and rust-coloured yellow ochres'. Though he had painted it in summer, he associated the work with the north. He painted another quarry in October 1889, but opted for the more colourful palette native to Japanese art in that case.

On 22 May 1889 Vincent wrote Theo that he had just drawn 'a large, rather rare moth, called a death's-head moth, with amazingly fine colours: black, grey, subtle white with a red reflection (or a hint of olive green). It is very large. To paint it I first had to kill it, which was a pity as it was such a beautiful animal'. Besides the drawing Vincent described, the Van Gogh Museum also preserves a sketch Vincent made of the same insect for Theo. In the definitive painting he portrayed it on an arum flower. There is also a superb reed pen study of a similar flower in the Museum.

Vincent van Gogh
Wheatfield with Reaper
Canvas, 73 × 92 cm - September 1889
Inv. S 49 V/1962 - F 618

On 2 July 1889 Vincent announced that he was working on a 'wheatfield with a small reaper and a large sun. The canvas is completely yellow, save for the wall and the background with purple hills'. After another attack interrupted him later that month he finally finished in September. Dissatisfied with the outcome, he plunged into the second version, shown here, which he finished around 4 September. Thinking his mother would be able to grasp the picture – 'as simple as one of those crude woodcuts you find in farmer's almanacs' – he made a smaller replica for her and his sister Wil (now in the Folkwang Museum, Essen). 'In this reaper – a vague figure working like the devil in the intense heat to finish his task – I then saw the image of death, in the sense that the wheat being reaped represents mankind. So if you will it's the opposite of the sower I've attempted in the past. But there's nothing sad about this death: it happens in broad daylight, under a sun that bathes everything in a fine, golden light'.

Vincent van Gogh
Reaper with Sickle
Canvas, 43.5 × 33.5 cm
Inv. S 198 V/1962 - F 687

The Sheaf-binder
Canvas, 43 × 33 cm
Inv. S 172 V/1962 - F 700

The Sheaf-binder
Canvas, 44.5 × 32 cm
Inv. S 173 V/1962 - F 693

Peasant Woman Beating Flax
Canvas, 40.5 × 26.5 cm
Inv. S 43 V/1962 - F 697

The Thresher
Canvas, 44 × 27 cm
Inv. S 171 V/1962 - F 692

The Sheep Shearers
Canvas, 43 × 29 cm
Inv. S 42 V/1962 - F 634

The Woodcutter
Canvas, 43.5 × 25 cm
Inv. S 170 V/1962 - F 670

A print by Adrien Lavieille after Millet with ten scenes of country life formed the inspiration for Vincent's series of as many small paintings, seven of which are still in the Van Gogh Museum. In a moment of crisis in September 1889 he sought to regain his bearings by copying the work of the French master. Most of the prints he copied meticulously, alternating the vertical formats at times with slightly more horizontal ones, and devising his own background for the sheaf-binder. Blue and yellow predominate, the two colours Vincent most associated with peasant life.

Vincent van Gogh
Window of Van Gogh's Studio in St Paul's
Hospital at St-Rémy
Black chalk and gouache, 62 × 47.6 cm - 1889
Inv. D 337 V/1962 - F 1528

Vincent van Gogh
The Vestibule of St Paul's Hospital at St-Rémy
Black chalk and gouache, 61.5 × 47.4 cm - 1889
Inv. D 176 V/1962 - F 1530

Vincent van Gogh
The Falling of the Leaves
Canvas, 73.5 × 60.5 cm - October 1889
Inv. S 46 V/1962 - F 651

Both of these paintings describe autumnal views of the garden of St Paul's Hospital at St-Rémy. The canvas with the lonely figure walking among tangled, Art Nouveau-like trees Vincent called *The Falling of the Leaves*. The work evinces painstaking observation, but also exemplifies Vincent's 'search for style [...] more virile and more powerful'.

Van Gogh described the large, sketch-like canvas with the garden of the asylum, which is actually the second version of the composition, in a letter to Emile Bernard: 'on the right a grey terrace, a bit of the house. Several overblown rosebushes, on the left the garden – red ochre – parched by the sun, covered with pine needles. The

edge of the garden is planted with large pines with red-ochre trunks and branches, as well as green foliage darkened with a mixture of black. The tall trees stand out against the evening sky in yellow intersected by purple stripes; the yellow becomes pink and green at the top. A wall – likewise red-ochre – obstructs the view and only

Vincent van Gogh
The Garden of St Paul's Hospital at St-Rémy
Canvas, 71.5 × 90.5 cm - December 1889
Inv. S 196 V/1962 - F 659

a purple and yellow-ochre hill rises above it. The first tree has an enormous trunk, but was struck by lightning and cut down. One branch, however, still sticks up very far and a rain of dark green needles is falling. That austere giant – his pride wounded – stands, if you give him the character of a human being, in contrast to the false smile of a last rose on the nearly overblown bush opposite it'.

A self-portrait of the tormented artist can be read into this description, yet the picture is also an implicit critique of themes recently painted by Gauguin and Bernard, which were far removed from visual reality. Van Gogh wanted to prove to them 'that you can express a feeling of anxiety without immediately referring to the historical Gethsemane'.

ST-RÉMY

Vincent van Gogh
The Plough and the Harrow (after Millet)
Canvas, 72 × 92 cm - January 1890
Inv. S 175 V/1962 - F 632

This copy after Millet is modelled on an etching by Alfred Delaunay. The composition can be traced to a picture Millet painted in three versions between 1862 and 1864, called *Winter: the Plain of Chailly*. The lack of figures distinguishes the work *vis-à-vis* the rest of Millet's oeuvre. The plough and harrow lying in the field are the only references to human activity, which came to a standstill in winter. Possibly because Delaunay's etching was unclear, the setting of Van Gogh's painting is more wintry than that of Millet's, and the effect even more desolate as a result. He blanketed the earth with a layer of snow and called the canvas *Le champ sous la neige*. In May 1890 Theo congratulated Vincent on the Millet copies, 'perhaps the most beautiful you've made'.

'I have the feeling that painting after those drawings by Millet is more a question of *translating them into another language* than of copying them', Vincent wrote his brother in November 1889. Theo concurred when he received the canvas in early January: 'Copied like this it is no longer a copy. There's a tone to it and everything is so beautifully surrounded with sky'.

The Evening Hour formed part of a set of four large pictures after Millet's *Heures de la journée*. Van Gogh painted the peasant interior – modelled again on a print by Lavieille – 'in a gamut of soft purples and lilacs'. He used bright colours to suggest radiant light within the dark interior, in contrast to the dark tonality of his Nuenen period, as exemplified by *The Potato Eaters*.

Possibly encouraged by the success of *The Evening Hour*, in late April 1890 Vincent considered 'redoing the picture of the peasants at table, by lamplight. By now that canvas must be altogether black; perhaps I can do it over completely from memory'.

Vincent van Gogh
A Small Stream in the Ravine, 'Les Peiroulets'
Canvas, 32 × 41 cm - October 1889
Inv. S 118 V/1962 - F 645

Vincent van Gogh
Bird's-eye View of an Olive Grove
Canvas, 33.5 × 40 cm - November/December 1889
Inv. S 148 V/1962 - F 716

Vincent van Gogh
Field with Two Rabbits
Canvas, 32.5 × 40.5 cm - autumn/winter 1889
Inv. S 99 V/1962 - F 739

The three oil studies illustrated here are among Van Gogh's lesser known works. Though somewhat exceptional within his oeuvre, they do have two things in common: all of them presumably date from the fourth quarter of 1889, and evince the author's abiding love for Japanese art, which survived his internment in St-Rémy.

Both chromatically and thematically, the brightly coloured brook in the ravine 'Les Peiroulets' is related to the large canvas *The Path through the Ravine* (of which there are versions in the Boston Museum of Fine Arts and the Rijksmuseum Kröller-Müller, Otterlo). Vincent associated the vivid colours of these works with Japan. He enjoyed the 'autumnal effects with their rich colouring, the green skies contrasting with yellow, orange and green trees and bushes, the bits of earth in every shade of purple [...]'.

In a letter to his friend Emile Bernard, Van Gogh remarked that his draughtsmanship and the large planes of colour which distinguished his work at the time occasionally recalled the artists of Pont-Aven. This certainly applies to the bird's-eye view of olive trees winding through a landscape. Here, the Japanese character is sooner determined by the decorative treatment of the subject than by the colour scheme. Playful rabbits in their natural surroun-dings are a motif that recurs frequently in Japonism. They figure, for instance, in prints by Henri Guérard, who illus-trated Louis Gonse's *L'Art Japonais*, and in those of Lucien Pissarro, whose wood engraving with rabbits belonged to the Van Gogh brothers' collection.

Vincent van Gogh
Olive Grove
Canvas, 73 × 92 cm - November 1889
Inv. S 45 V/1962 - F 707

While searching for 'somewhat contrasting effects of foliage, which constantly changes colour with the tints of the sky', Van Gogh produced no less than ten canvases with olive groves during his stay in St-Rémy. 'The effect of daylight, of sky is such that countless motifs can be gotten out of the olive trees', he wrote in May 1890. Irritated by the abstractions of his former comrades Gauguin and Bernard, in late 1889 he sought inspiration for his studies of olive groves in the work of Corot and Impressionists such as Monet and Renoir. In art he believed olive groves were destined to become an important theme: 'probably it won't be long before olive trees will be painted in every conceivable fashion, as the willow and the Dutch pollard willow have been, and the Norman apple tree ever since Daubigny and Cézar de Cock painted it'.

Vincent van Gogh
Pietà (after Delacroix)
Canvas, 73 × 60.5 cm - September 1889
Inv. S 168 V/1962 - F 630

Vincent van Gogh
The Raising of Lazarus (after Rembrandt)
Canvas, 50 × 65 cm - May 1890
Inv. S 169 V/1962 - F 677

In St-Rémy, Vincent copied not only after Millet, but after Daumier, Delacroix, Doré and Rembrandt as well. From Delacroix's oeuvre he chose the *Good Samaritan* and the *Pietà*. In describing his copy after the latter to his sister Wil, he wrote that the Mater Dolorosa had the 'good respectable hands of a working woman', and not an unfeeling, classical countenance, but 'the pale exterior, the vague, perplexed look of someone utterly exhausted by anxiety, weeping and sleeplessness'. In token of his recovery from a relapse in late February 1890, which had incapacitated him for two months, in May 1890 Vincent painted a canvas with an apposite biblical theme. The work is a free interpretation of a detail from Rembrandt's etching *The Raising of Lazarus*, which focuses on the reviving Lazarus and his two sisters. 'The cave and the corpse are violet, yellow and white. The woman removing the cloth from the face of the figure who's just been revived wears a green dress and has orange hair, while the other has black hair and wears a green-and- pink-striped dress. Behind them a landscape with blue hills and a yellow ascendant sun. As such the combination of colours has the same significance as the chiaroscuro of the etching'. Just as the Lazarus – like the Christ in the *Pietà* – is a thinly veiled self-portrait, both of the female figures unmistakeably represent Van Gogh's solicitous friends from Arles, Mesdames Ginoux and Roulin. Were they available as models, he wrote his brother, 'then I would certainly try and paint this canvas on a larger scale, since they resemble the [biblical] characters I imagined them to be'. Remarkably enough, the figure of Christ in Rembrandt's composition is replaced by the sun in Van Gogh's.

Like many of the other small canvases
in his oeuvre, this Alpilles landscape,
which entered the Museum in 1990 as
part of the Ribbius-Peletier Bequest, is
not mentioned in Van Gogh's
correspondence. It is usually dated to
June 1889, the period in which he painted
several large-scale versions of the same
landscape. Yet the fact that the trees at
the foot of the mountains are in bloom
suggests that it was actually made
months later, in the early spring of 1890.
After all, when Van Gogh arrived in
St-Rémy on 8 May 1889, the trees were
no longer flowering. The canvas
therefore must have been created at
about the same time as the *Almond
Branches in Blossom*, probably as a
colour study for a more ambitious work
which was never realised.

Vincent described the motif to his
brother shortly after being admitted to
the asylum on 22 May 1889: 'Through
the window with iron bars I can see an
enclosed wheatfield, a prospect similar
to a picture by Van Goyen'. In early June
he was already working on a large canvas
showing the view 'from the window of
my bedroom. In the foreground a
ruined cornfield that was beaten to the
ground by a thunderstorm. A wall as
enclosure and on the other side the grey
leaves of a few olive trees, cottages and
hills. [...] It is an extremely simple
landscape – also as regards colour'.

Just after the baby's birth on 31 January
1890, Theo informed his brother that he
was now the father of a healthy son
named Vincent Willem. On 9 February
he added that the child had blue eyes
'like the baby you painted with round
cheeks'. Vincent promptly painted a
picture for the proud parents' bedroom,
showing 'Large branches of almond
blossoms against a blue sky'. He
apparently drew inspiration from

Japanese prints, which so often contain
the same motif. While the artist was
briefly in Paris on 18 May 1890, en route
to Auvers, he enjoyed seeing his white
almond blossoms hanging above the
piano in his brother's apartment.

As in Arles, Van Gogh decided to
resume his series of blossoming trees
in St-Rémy in the spring of 1890, only to
have his plans frustrated once again by

illness. Having scarcely recovered from one attack, he was struck by another as he was finishing the illustrated canvas, which left him with no choice but to lay down his brush for two months. He could not have been more surprised by this latest setback, since he had just painted the almond blossoms 'with calm and meticulous brushwork'. Now he saw his hopes for the series dashed. 'I fell ill while working on the almond blossoms', he wrote his brother in April. 'Had I been able to continue, you can well imagine I would have done more trees in blossom'. 'Now the trees have all but stopped blossoming; really, I have no luck'.

Vincent van Gogh
Cottages and Cypresses Beneath a Stormy Sky
Canvas on panel, 29 × 36.5 cm - March/April 1890
Inv. S 112 V/1962 - F 675

Though Van Gogh usually stopped working whenever he was ill, he made countless drawings after Brabant motifs during the attack of March-April 1890, thus expressing his nostalgia for the north. As he wrote his mother and sister in late April, 'while my illness was at its worst, I carried on painting regardless, including a souvenir of Brabant, cottages with moss roofs and copses of beech, on an autumn evening with stormy sky, the red sun setting in reddish clouds'. He made these 'souvenirs of the north' from memory, but asked his brother and mother to send him old studies and drawings for inspiration. 'Though they are not good

in and of themselves, they can help me remember things and serve as material for new work'. He kept his word while staying in Auvers, where he painted new versions of such Nuenen themes as *The Cottage* and *The Church Tower*. The cypresses are especially striking in this 'Souvenir du Nord'. Aside from olive trees, Van Gogh considered them the pre-eminent symbol of Provence: 'with respect to line and proportion, every bit as beautiful as an Egyptian obelisk. And the green is so extraordinary. It is the *black* note in a sunny landscape, but it is one of the most interesting black notes, so far as I can imagine one of the most difficult to get down on canvas well. You

should see them here against the blue, or rather *in* the blue'.
The critic Albert Aurier made some flattering remarks about Vincent's cypresses – 'their silhouettes pointing upward like nightmares of black flame' – in an article that appeared in January 1890. In gratitude, the artist presented him with one of his most ambitious treatments of the motif, which is now in the Rijksmuseum Kröller-Müller. He had already started working on the canvas in the summer of 1889, but been interrupted by an attack in July. The smaller of the two pictures illustrated here is a replica of it.

Vincent van Gogh
The Cypresses
Canvas, 43.5 × 27 cm -
February 1890
Inv. S 147 V/1962 - F 621

In early June Van Gogh wrote from Auvers that he had been 'working very hard lately in St-Rémy, on floral bouquets in particular: roses and purple irises'. Altogether he painted four large flower pieces, possibly hoping to match the success he had achieved with a similar picture of irises at the Salon des Indépendants. *Vase with Irises* is an excellent example of 'enormously divergent complementary colours, which stand out all the more strongly because of their contrasts'. The three small nature studies, which once more betray strong Japanese influence, date from the same spring.

Vincent van Gogh
Wild Roses
Canvas, 24.5 × 33 cm -
Inv. S 190 V/1962 - F 597

Vincent van Gogh
Butterflies and Poppies
Canvas, 34.5 × 25.5 cm -
Inv. S 188 V/1962 - F 748

Vincent van Gogh
Roses and a Beetle
Canvas, 33.5 × 24.5 cm
Inv. S187 V/1962 - F 749

Vincent van Gogh
Vase with Irises against a Yellow Background
Canvas, 92 × 73.5 cm - May 1890
Inv. S 50 V/1962 - F 678

Vincent van Gogh
Ears of Wheat
Canvas, 64.5 × 48.5 cm - June 1890
Inv. S 88 V/1962 - F 767

Van Gogh in Auvers

The last seventy days of his life Vincent van Gogh spent just north of Paris in the small town of Auvers-sur-Oise. More than once the artist had expressed his longing for the north while still living in St-Rémy. After lengthy correspondence on the subject with Theo he finally settled on Auvers, where the physician Paul Gachet would keep an eye on him. Alongside his medical practice Gachet also did a bit of painting. He and Monticelli had been friends, and his collection testified to his contact with such artists as Cézanne, Guillaumin, Pissarro and Renoir.

It was Dr Gachet who also introduced Vincent to the art of etching; the ensuing experiments resulted in an etched portrait of Gachet. Though they only lay some thirty kilometres from Paris and were popular with Parisians, Auvers and nearby Pontoise were known primarily as rural art colonies. Besides the aforementioned Cézanne and Pissarro, Daubigny had lived and worked there as well. The extraordinarily large number of paintings, drawings and sketchbook scribblings Van Gogh produced during this period attest to his inquisitiveness about his new surroundings, which were 'of a grave beauty'.

The long crisis he had endured between February and April 1890 in St-Rémy certainly made him no less susceptibile to new impressions, depicting both the picturesque village and the wheatfields in the outstretched landscape of the Ile-de-France. He used the 'close-up' of cornstalks as a background for a study of a peasant girl, inspired by his lifelong models Millet and Breton. In a letter to Gauguin of mid-June 1890 he described the painting: 'nothing but ears of corn, greenish-blue stalks, long, ribbon-like leaves, green and pink on account of the reflection [...]. They are greens of varying quality, of the same colour value, so that they form a green entity which owing to the vibration recalls the soft noises of the ears of corn swaying back and forth in the wind'.

Vincent van Gogh
Portrait of Dr Paul
Gachet
'L'homme à la pipe'
Etching 18 × 15 cm -
June 1890
Inv. P 469 V/1962 -
F 1664

Travelling from Paris Vincent reached Auvers on 20 May. Three days later he wrote his brother that he was 'doing very well these days. I'm working hard, and have done four painted studies and two drawings. You'll see a drawing of an old vineyard with the figure of a peasant woman which I'm thinking of turning into a large canvas'. The two drawings have been kept together and are now in the Van Gogh Museum. Though his plans for a painted version of the *Old Vineyard with Peasant Woman* apparently came to naught, he did produce several canvases showing the picturesque houses of Auvers. The two illustrated drawings have been called 'symphonies in purple-blue'. It is not

Vincent van Gogh
Landscape with Cottages
Pencil and watercolour, 45 × 54.5 cm - May 1890
Inv. D 332 V/1962 - F 1640 r

clear, however, what inspired Van Gogh's use of the shade, since there is no longer any trace of it in his painted versions of such motifs. Both drawings were executed vigorously *en plein air* and later retouched in the studio. The drawings perpetuate the theme of thatched-roof cottages from Vincent's 'Souvenirs du Nord'. No sooner had he arrived in Auvers than he noticed them: 'Auvers is very beautiful – among other things [there are] many thatched roofs, something that's becoming rare. By doing a few canvases of them very conscientiously I hope to have some chance of covering my living expenses [...] it's truly rural, characteristic and picturesque'.

Vincent van Gogh
Old Vineyard with Peasant Woman
Pencil and watercolour, 43.5 × 54 cm - May 1890
Inv. D 446 V/1962 - F 1624

Vincent van Gogh
View of Auvers
Canvas, 50 × 52 cm - May/June 1890
Inv. S 105 V/1962 - F 799

Auvers was very popular with painters. On Corot's advice, Daubigny had settled there in the late 1850s; in the '70s, the Impressionists Guillaumin and Pissarro spent time there as well. In the collection of his friend Dr Gachet, Van Gogh could see for himself how Cézanne had previously portrayed the town and artists were still working in Auvers by the time Vincent arrived. While it is true he narrowly missed the French painter Louis Dumoulin, who was known for his 'Japanese work', he was able to spend several days with Walpole Brooke; having grown up in Japan, the Australian artist must have fascinated the Dutchman.

So much did Vincent enjoy the tranquil village that he tried to convince Theo to leave Paris, thinking it would do him good – be it for only a month – to bring his family and enjoy the 'peacefulness à la Puvis de Chavannes'. As if to entice his brother he noted the 'numerous villas and modern bourgeois houses, very gay in the sun with lots of flowers'.

Shortly after arriving in Auvers, Vincent wrote his brother 'Word has it that Mme Daubigny and Mme Daumier still live here – at least I know for certain the former does'. Daubigny, one of Van Gogh's favourite painters, had built a house in Auvers in 1861, where indeed his widow still resided. As early as 17 June the Dutch artist had 'an idea for a larger canvas of Daubigny's house and garden, of which I've already done a small study'. That study has much in common with the Impressionists' handling of such garden scenes. Yet it was not till late July that Theo was shown a sketch of the completed work, in the last letter he was to receive from his brother.

Vincent made two versions of *Daubigny's Garden*, which he himself considered one of his 'most intensely felt works'. Both are painted on horizontal canvases measuring 50 x 100 cm, a format he alone employed in Auvers. For this particular study, showing only the right half of the definitive composition, he chose a square canvas exactly half that size.

Vincent van Gogh
The Garden of Daubigny (study
Canvas, 50.7 × 50.7 cm - June 18
Inv. S 104 V/1962 - F 765

The series of large bouquets of roses and irises he painted just before leaving St-Rémy was Van Gogh's last major project in this genre. Most of the still lifes he produced in Auvers are modest studies, which for all their simplicity make a nonetheless daring impression. Their composition is usually very informal and surprisingly modern. The illustrated still life is one of the most peaceful in the series; it reiterates the composition of the large still lifes *Sunflowers* and *Irises* on a smaller scale. The manner seems to have been influenced by a flower piece Cézanne painted in 1873 which belonged to Dr Gachet. The work now hangs in the Musée d'Orsay, Paris.

Vincent van Gogh
House with Two Figures
Canvas, 38 × 45 cm - May/June 1890
Inv. S 108 V/1962 - F 806

Vincent van Gogh
Vase with Flowers
Canvas, 42 × 29 cm - June 1890
Inv. S 109 V/1962 - F 764a

Vincent van Gogh
Two Pear Trees with the Château of Auvers
Canvas, 50 × 101 cm · June 1890
Inv. S 107 V/1962 · F 770

When it came to architecture, Van Gogh rarely tried his hand at anything grandiose. His taste ran to humble cottages on the whole, and when he chose religious architecture as a motif, he generally preferred village churches over cathedrals. In Arles, for instance, he ignored virtually all the architecture of note, including the imposing Roman ruins. It was exactly the same story in Auvers: aside from the local church and the small town hall, he confined himself to modest vernacular architecture. At first glance the illustrated canvas with the seventeenth-century château of Auvers appears to be an exception to the rule, but on closer inspection it becomes clear that the summer evening, not the château, is the subject. Vincent described the picture, which he finished shortly before 24 June, as 'an evening effect: two pear trees completely black against a yellowing sky, with cornfields and in the purple background the château surrounded by dark foliage'. The composition resembles an elongated version of one of the last blossoming orchards he painted in Arles, just as the charged, melancholic atmosphere and the silhouette-like forms recall some of his desolate Drenthe and Nuenen landscapes. Van Gogh may have been thinking of Charles Daubigny, who specialised in evocative landscapes at dusk. Indeed he could have seen many of the French master's works in the collection of the Hague painter-collector Willem Mesdag, which comprised more Daubignys than any other outside France.

Vincent van Gogh
Wheatfields Beneath Thunderclouds
Canvas, 50 × 100.5 cm - July 1890
Inv. S 106 V/1962 - F 778

Vincent van Gogh
Crows in the Wheatfields
Canvas, 50.5 × 103 cm - July 1890
Inv. S 149 V/1962 - F 779

When Vincent briefly visited Paris on 6 July 1890, Theo informed him he was contemplating leaving Boussod & Valadon and going into business for himself. Vincent already had qualms about burdening his brother, and now that Theo's plans threatened his precarious finances, the situation became unbearable. Theo's wife Jo sought to reassure her disconsolate brother-in-law, to which he responded around 10 July:

'My dear brother and sister, Jo's letter was really like a gospel to me, a deliverance from the agony caused by the hours I'd shared with you, which were a bit too difficult and trying for us all. It was quite something when we all felt our daily bread was in danger, quite something when we realised that for other reasons as well our existence is so vulnerable. Back here, I was still very

sad and continued to feel the storm that threatens you weighing on me, too. What can we do? I generally try to be fairly cheerful, you know, but the very foundation of my life is also threatened, and now my situation is likewise insecure'. Though he himself claimed the brush nearly fell from his hand, back in Auvers Van Gogh painted two 'enormous outstretched wheatfields beneath angry skies, and I have consciously tried to express sadness and extreme loneliness in them'. These landscapes with heavily overcast skies have inspired the most disparate interpretations. Especially because the *Wheatfield with Crows* was long mistaken for Van Gogh's last work, it has been seen as a premonition of his suicide on 29 July 1890. Yet the true tenor of these works is altogether different, and – notwithstanding the

gloom – positive: 'I'm all but certain that in those canvases I have formulated what I cannot express in words, namely how healthy and heartening I find the countryside'. The landscapes belong to a series of twelve canvases of the same horizontal format, collectively forming a paen to country life. As such, the cycle fulfilled an ambition the artist had cherished even before leaving Holland. The Art Nouveau-like canvas with the tortured tree roots is an astonishingly modern, almost abstract work. Yet it is not the first of its kind in Vincent's oeuvre. It was preceded by the drawing *Les Racines*, executed during his Hague period in 1882, which was an attempt to visualise 'the struggle of life'.

Vincent van Gogh
Tree Roots
Canvas, 50 × 100 cm - July 1890
Inv. S 195 V/1962 - F 816

Joseph Mendes da Costa
Amsterdam 1863 - 1939 Amsterdam
Vincent van Gogh
Bronze, 13.5 × 39 cm
Inv. V 49 V/1981

Fin-de-siècle

This last chapter shows the development of the visual arts in both of Vincent van Gogh's native countries, namely the Netherlands and France, during the period 1890-1914. The *fin-de-siècle* was dominated by Symbolism, an artistic movement that drew much of its inspiration from literature and esoteric religious movements. Symbolists placed a higher priority on the representation of abstract ideas than on observable reality. Following her brother-in-law's death in July 1890 and then her husband's in January 1891, Jo van Gogh was left in Paris with the brothers' collection as well as the sizeable legacy of Vincent's paintings and drawings. She eventually decided to take her infant son Vincent Willem and the whole collection with her to the Netherlands. At that point she threw herself into promoting the art of her late brother-in-law, lending his work to numerous exhibitions, those at the Haagsche Kunstkring in 1892 and Amsterdam's Stedelijk Museum in 1905 being only the most important. Through the German dealer Paul Cassirer, Vincent's work was also shown repeatedly in Germany, where it attracted a great many collectors. In

1914, moreover, Jo's edition of Vincent's letters to Theo appeared and was subsequently translated into other languages. After her death in 1925, her son continued where Jo left off. The mythology surrounding Van Gogh would have it that his genius was utterly misunderstood at the time of his death. The tragedy, rather, was that his death coincided with his breakthrough. The fact is that Vincent's work was favourably received at exhibitions in Paris and Brussels while he was still alive, as evidenced by the enthusiastic review written by Albert Aurier. After his death,

the artists Emile Bernard in France and Jan Toorop in the Netherlands joined Jo van Gogh in fostering the fame of the late artist. Thanks in part to their efforts, his oeuvre was regularly exhibited in the 1890s and inspired many young artists. Around the turn of the century, when Impressionism experienced a second florescence, the so-called 'Fauves' in France and the German Expressionists let themselves be influenced by the work of Van Gogh. Along with Gauguin, Seurat and Cézanne, the Dutch master was now proclaimed one of the 'fathers of modern art'.

Johan Cohen Gosschalk
Zwolle 1873-1912 Amsterdam
Portrait of Jo van Gogh-Bonger
Pencil and coloured chalk, 37 × 27 cm - 1902
Inv. D 791 T/1982

Though there was nothing ambiguous about Van Gogh's attitude toward the direction Bernard's art took in the late 1880s – the Dutchman's last letters to his friend were extremely critical – Bernard continued working on his friend's behalf even after his death. The Frenchman was instrumental in organising a memorial exhibition at Theo's apartment in Paris and in April 1892 he put together a modest retrospective exhibition at the gallery of Le Barc de Boutteville. Bernard himself produced a catalogue of the latter in the form of a woodcut, of which only a few exemplars survive. It lists a total of sixteen pictures, only twelve of which were actually displayed.

Emile Bernard
Lille 1868-1941 Paris
Catalogue of the Van Gogh exhibition at Le Barc de Boutteville
Wood engraving, 40.3 × 30.8 cm - 1891/92
Inv. P 530 V/1990

Emile Bernard
Still Life with Cup, Fruit Bowl, Teapot and Fruit
Canvas, 39 × 47 cm - 1890
Inv. S 395 M/1990, presented by Elin Ekström

Following the deaths of Vincent and Theo van Gogh in 1890 and 1891, Bernard stayed in touch with the Netherlands. He did so primarily through Theo's brother-in-law Andries Bonger, who had accumulated a large collection of his work. The *Still Life with Cup, Fruit Bowl, Teapot and Fruit* of 1890, which Bernard dedicated to the collector, is remarkably dynamic. The steep slant of the table lends a sense of movement to the composition and the objects themselves seem animated. The effect recalls Ravel's *L'Enfant et les sortilèges*.

In the late 1880s historical, one might even say 'romantic' motifs suddenly appeared in Bernard's work, many of which can be traced to the Middle Ages. His manner is reminiscent of tapestries, owing perhaps to the artist's former connection to the textile industry of his native Lille. Indeed it was during this same period that Bernard became increasingly involved with applied art.

The subject of the painting *The Blue Bird* derives from the artist's childhood. An autobiographical note he sent Emile Schuffenecker in 1891 includes the following poem:

I had no friends
Sat at the head of my small bed
Pale and feverish
I dreamt of music
I read large picture books
Full of enchanted fairytales
The Sleeping Beauty who sleeps
In a bed fit for a wise king
The Blue Bird swooping through the street
Like a magic carpet.

Emile Bernard
The Blue Bird
Canvas, 76 × 60 cm - 1889
Inv. S 393 M/1990, presented by Elin Ekström

Emile Bernard
Pont-Aven Seen from the Bois d'Amour
Canvas, 101 × 76 cm - 1892
Inv. S 293 V/1969

In 1886 Bernard became acquainted with the work of Cézanne, whose influence was already sporadically manifest in his pictures. The impact of the older artist is unmistakeable in this hunting scene, painted around 1889. While the subject recalls the classical myth of the Calydonian boar, the style is reminiscent of a sylvan scene by Cézanne that once belonged to Van Gogh's brother-in-law Andries Bonger, now in the Rijksmuseum Kröller-Müller.

The view of Pont-Aven of 1892 likewise derives from the Bonger Collection. In the early 1890s Bernard was no less inspired by the landscape of Brittany than he had ever been. But rather than the stylised forms of the School of Pont-Aven, the palette and manner of Cézanne clearly exercised the greatest influence on his style once again. As the artist put it in a letter to Andries Bonger of 1891, 'Chacun a son maître décidément et s'y conforme au possible – moi j'ai Cézanne'. Bernard did not actually meet the master from Aix in person until 1904, on returning from Egypt. In that period he painted several still lifes under Cézanne's guidance and, in July 1904, published an article to which we owe much of our knowledge about him. Following a second encounter in 1905 Bernard published two more 'Souvenirs sur Paul Cézanne' in October 1907.

Emile Bernard
Landscape with Hunters
Canvas, 73 × 50 cm - ca. 1889
Inv. S 397 M/1990, presented by Elin Ekström

Odilon Redon
Bordeaux 1840-1916 Paris
The Village of Samois
Oil on paper, 42.9 × 30.3 cm - 1888
Inv. S 436 M/1992

Odilon Redon was known for his mysterious, mystical lithographs and charcoal drawings of mythical creatures and other imaginary subjects. Nevertheless, the origins of his art lay primarily in nature. As he put it in his *A Soi-Même*, 'Leaving the city, going into the fields, approaching a small village in all its rustic peacefulness, that always made my heart race, which sobered me and, having abruptly returned to myself, made me stammer distractedly that living there was truly living – perhaps'. The notable chiaroscuro in this village scene recalls Corot, whom Redon considered 'the most poetic interpreter of the contemporary landscape'. Like him, Redon felt like a 'painter eye to eye with nature, a poet or a thinker in his studio'. While the work of the older artist generally evokes nostalgia, Redon's emanates a mystical tranquillity. Small French towns in midsummer can often seem desolate, and this quiet street anticipates the 'villes mortes' that would so fascinate the later Symbolists. *Village Street in Samois* is one of the seventy-five personal 'études pour l'auteur' with which Redon never wished to part. Only after the artist's death did his widow Camille consign it to the Haarlem gallery of De Bois. Indeed it was through this dealer that much of Redon's work would find its way into Dutch collections. In 1915, De Bois published Redon's complete graphic oeuvre, to the artist's 'profound satisfaction'. For years De Bois also dealt in Van Gogh on behalf of the late artist's sister-in-law Jo.

The Van Gogh Museum preserves three pastels by Odilon Redon, all of which derive from the collection of Andries Bonger, Theo van Gogh's brother-in-law. The two men had met in Paris in 1881, and it was through Theo van Gogh that Bonger became acquainted with Emile Bernard. Bernard, in turn, put Bonger in touch with Redon in 1891. Though the collector always remained loyal to Bernard, his enthusiasm for Redon's art – 'the passion of my life' – eclipsed his taste for Bernard's in the long run.

Vierge nimbée may possibly represent the Virgin Mary as Stella Maris (Star of the Sea), the patron saint of seamen. Redon's own description of the work survives: 'Dark brown sky with purple and red clouds; on the left a being with a halo on a barque, gold hawsers by the bow of the barque, and over the water a kind of luminous blue like a will-o'-the-wisp'.

Bonger acquired *Vierge nimbée* from the collection of the sculptress Saar de Swart in 1902. Along with the poet Ary Prins and the painter Isaac Israëls, De Swart was one of the earliest collectors of Redon's work in the Netherlands. She had received the pastel from the artist himself as a gift in December 1898.

Odilon Redon
Vierge nimbée
Pastel, 44.2 × 28 cm - ca. 1898
Inv. D 809 M/1986, acquired with the support of the Vereniging Rembrandt

Odilon Redon
Portrait of Madame Camille Redon and her
Son Arï
Pastel, 59.3 × 43.6 cm - ca. 1903
Inv. D 811 M/1987

Around 1908 Andries Bonger purchased
this double portrait of Redon's wife and
son directly from the artist. The highly
abstracted figures are not unlike the
women in Maurice Denis's *The Two
Sisters*. In his portraits, Redon sought to
'represent only the character of a
human being, his character as such',
rather than the sitter's outer
appearance. He considered this 'the
ultimate and highest task of the painter'.

Maurice Denis
Granville 1870-1943 Paris
The Two Sisters
Canvas, 40.5 × 32.5 cm - 1891
Inv. S 423 V/1991

Denis was one of the charter members
of the Nabis, the group of artists formed
in 1888, for whom he wrote a manifesto
in August 1890. In that context he made
his famous pronouncement that a
picture, 'before being a horse, a nude or
an anecdotal subject, is essentially a flat
surface covered with colours arranged
in a certain order'. For Denis, painting
was not about imitating nature
faithfully, but about expressing an 'état
d'âme' by freely employing colour and
line. He thus affirmed recent
developments in Symbolist literature.
The canvas with the two mysterious
women was long known as 'Les deux
japonaises', until it was recognised as a
fragment of a larger canvas inspired by
Maurice Maeterlinck's play *L'Intruse*.
The entire composition is known
through a lithograph after it by Paul
Fort, which appeared in the programme
printed for the première of the piece in
the Théâtre d'Art on 20 May 1891. Since
it had apparently been difficult to sell in
its original form, the artist decided to
delete several fragments. The two
women in our canvas formed the centre
of the original composition. Denis
himself is responsible for the floral
motifs on the frame, which are
reminiscent of Japanese prints.

Odilon Redon
Bordeaux 1840-1916 Paris
Vase with Flowers
Pastel, 60.5 × 47.5 cm
Inv. D 688 V/1962

Symbolist artists displayed a definite predilection for floral motifs. Not only their paintings and drawings but also their designs for posters and applied art are distinguished by profuse vegetation, with lush flowers and plants in decorative arrangements growing luxuriantly over surfaces. It was certainly no coincidence that the controversial Symbolist artists associated with Joséphin 'Sâr' Peladan and his 'Salon de la Rose+Croix' incorporated a flower in their coat of arms.

In the early work of Odilon Redon flowers already play a prominent role. Like the 'flower girls' (*Blumenmädchen*) in Wagner's opera *Parsifal*, the 'fleurs étranges' in his lithos and charcoal drawings often have human faces. Far from charming or reassuring, they are rather 'fleurs du mal', inspired by the homonymous collection of poems by Charles Baudelaire. In the 1890s, however, Redon's palette brightened considerably and the floral motifs, now arranged somewhat more traditionally in bouquets, are more appealing.

Most of the pastel flower pieces were produced during the last twenty years of Redon's career. In this period his work became increasingly colourful and he studied nature more intensively. This is not to say that he imitated nature slavishly – as the Impressionists did in his eyes. Redon's bouquets float in a space that is entirely undefined; having no relation to any physical context, they are utterly absorbed in their own game of subtle gradations of colour. Even a picture of a simple apple should suggest 'une ambiance de pensées autour d'elle', Redon believed. This explains how yet another flower piece Andries Bonger purchased from Redon, could be entitled *Vision*.

The illustrated pastel also derives from the collection of Andries Bonger.

Symbolist artists often imputed a deeper meaning to the flowers in their works. This was nothing new at the time. Van Gogh's sunflowers were meant to symbolise Hope, just as the lily is a traditional Christian token of purity and chastity, and therefore often associated with the Virgin Mary.

In this watercolour by the Swiss artist Carlos Schwabe, a path of lilies forming a bridge between heaven and earth constitutes the central motif. Along it the Madonna holding her Son is seen descending to earth.

Schwabe received his initial training at the Ecole des Arts in Geneva. There he devoted himself to minute drawings in watercolour, which became his specialty. After settling in Paris, his work caught the attention of Joséphin Péladan, who invited the artist to take part in his first Salon de la Rose+Croix in 1892 and to make the poster for it. In that design lilies also play a prominent role, bordering the path along which a personification of the Faith is led upwards to the Kingdom of the Ideal by the figure of ethereal Purity.

Of Schwabe's Madonna with the lilies two versions exist, this being the larger of the two. In 1899 the critic Gustave Soulier briefly summarised his impression of Schwabe's lilies: 'The plants in his work are more human: he always expresses that brotherhood between all creatures'. Just as neatly he described 'the image of that lily path growing in the clouds, through which strides the Virgin: white blossoms sprung from whites, a harmony of the most radiant forms of creation. The path is at once an enclosure that protects her and an offering that rises round her, compassion that encircles her and a supplicant caressing [...]'.

Carlos Schwabe
Altona 1866-1926 Davon
La Vierge aux Lys (Virgin of the Lilies)
Watercolour, 97 × 49 cm - 1899
Inv. D 1037 M/1993

Eugène Carrière
Gournay 1849-1906 Paris
Portrait of Arthur Fontaine and his Daughter
Canvas, 128 × 96.5 cm - ca. 1903
Inv. S 440 V/1993

_____

_____

Albert Besnard
Paris 1849-1934 Paris
The Departure
Canvas, 30 × 46 cm
Inv. S 208 V/1962

These pages illustrate three dreamy fin-de-siècle portraits. Edmond Aman-Jean, friend and model of Georges Seurat, with whom he shared a studio for some time, studied at the Ecole des Beaux-Arts and under Puvis de Chavannes. His strength lay in poetic portraits of women. This intimate canvas shows the woman he would marry in 1892.

The reputation of Albert Besnard likewise rests on society portraits, often done in pastel. Though his style occasionally verges on Impressionism, Degas and Pissarro were concerned that he compromised their principles by pandering to popular taste. It was at the Salon of 1885 that Besnard first attracted the attention of Theo van Gogh, who would help the artist out of financial difficulties several years hence. Theo may have received this canvas from the artist as a token of gratitude. The pronounced English character of the work could be explained by the fact that Besnard worked in England between 1880 and 1882.

Eugène Carrière was also acquainted with Theo van Gogh. Following the death of the dealer's brother Vincent, Carrière sent a letter of condolence to Theo, whom he may have met through his friend Gauguin.

The sitter, Arthur Fontaine, was a brother-in-law of the composer Chausson, and a friend of Debussy as well as such writers as Gide and Claudel. Several years earlier he had also sat for Redon. The double portrait focuses on Carrière's paternity, contrasting the father's introverted expression with the more outgoing character of the daughter. The two vague, monochromatic figures seem to be surrounded by a mystical fluïdium, in keeping with Carrière's determination to capture an abstract emotion, or 'état d'âme'.

Edmond-François Aman-Jean
Chevry-Cossigny 1860-1935 Paris
Portrait of Thadée Caroline Jacquet
Canvas, 55.2 × 46.1 cm - ca. 1892
Inv. S 420 M/1991

Louis Welden Hawkins
Esslingen 1849-1910 Paris
Innocence
Canvas, 73 × 50.2 cm
Inv. S 427 M/1991

_____

Though born in the vicinity of Stuttgart and of British descent – he was related to the English critic George Moore – Hawkins spent most of his active life in Paris and took French citizenship in 1895. He received his artistic training at the Académie Julian under William Bouguereau and Jules Lefebvre, and began exhibiting at the Salon in 1881. For some time he worked in the Naturalist style of Bastien-Lepage, before developing his own, remarkably personal manner. In the 1890s Hawkins concentrated on allegorical figure pieces, to which he assigned such titles as *Matérialisme et Idéalisme* and *Noë – toile mystique*. At that time he belonged to the literary circle that centred round the Symbolists Mallarmé and De Montesquiou, was friendly with Puvis de Chavannes, Rodin and Carrière, and figured prominently in the exhibitions of the Rose+Croix and Libre Esthétique. As well as to their esoteric subject matter, Hawkins's minutely painted canvases owe their beguiling, highly unusual appearance to their combination of a linear manner with gold and monochrome. *Innocence* betrays the influence of the Italian Renaissance, and in the background there are apocalyptic motifs derived from a print by Dürer. Around 1900 Hawkins abandoned the Symbolist idiom in favour of Impressionist land- and cityscapes. His self-portrait of 1906 is a moving document of the ageing artist. After a career which must have had its share of disappointment, he seems to take a hard look at his ambitions and to weigh the pros and cons of an artist's life without flinching.

Louis Welden Hawkins
Self-portrait
Canvas, 80 × 72.5 cm - 1906
Inv. S 435 M/1993

reminiscent of pictures by Leonardo.
A study for Point's homonymous picture
of the same size – the pastel *The Siren* is
dedicated to the Symbolist poet Henri
de Regnier (1864-1936).
Emile Bernard, who had turned his
back on the avant-garde around the
turn of the century and begun working
in a classicist style, praised Point in an
article of 1906 as 'one of the first, if not
the first, among the Innovators of Art
who has gone back to the sources,
plumbed their depths and courageously
brought back a glass of that wondrous
water which, with its diamond-like
clarity, forms the mirror so beloved of
the gods'.

Armand Point
Algiers 1860-1932
Paris
La Sirène
Pastel, 91.4 × 71.8 cm -
1897
Dedicated to Henri de
Regnier
Inv. D 1039 M/1993

Like Hawkins, the French Symbolist
Armand Point was fascinated by the
'femme fatale'. Here he visualises one
of the Sirens whose song – according to
classical Greek mythology – lured
sailors to their deaths upon the rocks.
The Greek hero Odysseus craftily
escaped this fate. Reluctant to miss the
song of the Sirens – of which there were
originally two according to the myth –
but mindful of the danger involved, he
had himself bound to the mast of his
ship and stopped the ears of his
companions with wax.
Like Hawkins, Armand Point drew
inspiration from the art of the Italian
Renaissance and the English Pre-
Raphaelites. In 1894 he visited Italy,
where he was impressed by the work of
Botticelli and Leonardo da Vinci. The
Siren's complicated headdress is clearly

Fernand Khnopff
Grembergen-bij-Dendermonde 1858-1921
Brussels
Portrait of the Violinist Achille Lerminiaux
Pastel, pencil and gum on paper,
16.6 × 16.6 cm - 1885
Inv. D 911 M/1989

Octave Maus, the business manager of
the Brussels artist's association Les XX,
was quick to recognise the importance
of Vincent van Gogh and invited the
Dutchman to exhibit several pictures in
1889, thus contributing significantly to
his breakthrough. A female member of
the group – the painter Anna Boch – was
the first to purchase one of Vincent's
pictures, moreover. This influential
gathering of Belgian avant-gardists also
included James Ensor, Fernand
Khnopff, Theo van Rijsselberghe,
Félicien Rops and Henry van de Velde.
Dutch artists such as George Breitner,
Isaac Israëls and Floris Verster were
invited to exhibit at Les XX, while Jan
Toorop was actually a member.
The Belgian Symbolist Fernand Khnopff
studied under Xavier Mellery in Bruges
for some time, and was influenced by
the work of Eugène Delacroix and
Gustave Moreau in Paris. Described as
an intellectual dandy, he was famous
for depicting *femmes fatales* with
sphinx- or Medusa-like features.
Khnopff was also a fine portrait painter.
As such he preferred to work in pastel,
which is ideally suited to obscure,
mystical effects. His portrait of 1885
shows the violinist Achille Lerminiaux
with eyes closed, absorbed in a private
dialogue with his Muse.

George Minne
Ghent 1866-1941 Latem
Solidarity
Bronze, 66.5 × 66.5 × 27 cm - 1898
Inv. V/91 V/1993

Jan Toorop's self-portrait of 1883 shows the 25-year-old artist as a true bohemian, surrounded by the attributes of his art. Self-confident to the point of arrogance, he is clearly on the threshold of a brilliant career. Born in the Dutch East Indies, Toorop was one of the most internationally oriented Dutch artists of the *fin-de-siècle*. In the course of the 1880s he rapidly absorbed such divergent trends as Realism and a brand of Impressionism heavily indebted to Manet and Neo-impressionism, of which he was the earliest exponent in the Netherlands. In Belgium, Toorop associated with Whistler and the Belgian avant-garde (becoming a member of Les XX in 1884). In the 1890s he chaired the painting division of the artists' association known as the 'Haagsche Kunstkring'; as such he was the driving force behind the first major Van Gogh exhibition in the Netherlands in 1892. His present reputation is largely based on the Symbolist works he produced after 1890.

The Belgian sculptor George Minne, a friend of the poets Maeterlinck and Verhaeren, exhibited at both Les XX and the Salons de la Rose+Croix. His sculpture *Solidarité*, also known under the title *La barque humaine*, is a smaller version in bronze of what was originally conceived as a monument to the Belgian socialist Jean Volders, but never realised. Minne's inimitable, fragile art lends a certain monumentality to tender human emotions.

Jan Toorop
Poerworedjo 1858-1928 The Hague
Self-portrait in Studio
Canvas, 50.8 × 36.3 cm - 1883
Inv. S 388 M/1989

George Hendrik Breitner
Rotterdam 1857-1923 Amsterdam
Girl in the Grass
Watercolour, 26 × 27 cm - 1880
Inv. D 726 V/1961

Of the painters who set the pace in Holland between 1890 and the Great War, Breitner was the only one with whom Van Gogh had been personally acquainted. In 1882 the two artists would often amble through The Hague looking for types of figures with a view to studying them from the model. Yet Vincent did not always hold his comrade in high regard. In July 1883, for instance, he saw three 'indigestible' pieces in Breitner's atelier: 'patches of faded colour on a bleached, dusty and mouldy wallpaper, as it were'. Breitner's 'studies of common girls of the street' he found 'infinitely better'. Like Van Gogh, Breitner worked for a while in Paris in Cormon's studio. In 1886 he moved to Amsterdam, where he became the leader of the so-called 'Amsterdam Impressionists'. The pastel *Two Amsterdam Girls* depicts just the sort of 'common girls of the street' Van Gogh had in mind. It is difficult to imagine a contrast greater than that between this pastel and Breitner's *Girl in the Grass* of ten years earlier, a delicate watercolour from the collection of Theo van Gogh.

In 1889 Breitner wrote Floris Verster that 'If I had money, I'd buy the poppies'. He had just been admiring his colleague's monumental still life in a show in Amsterdam, where the canvas was hailed as the 'triumphant shout' of the avant-garde. Far removed from his rowdy confrères in Amsterdam, Verster led a solitary existence in Leiden. Though he did not know Van Gogh personally, he later came to admire the older artist's work, and shared his inclination to heighten colour and assign symbolic value to observed reality.

George Hendrik Breitner
Two Amsterdam Girls
Pastel, 50 × 40 cm - ca. 1890
Inv. D 1005 M/1990

Floris Verster
Leiden 1861-1927
Leiden
Japanese Poppies
Canvas, 163 × 101.5 cm
1888
Inv. S 413 M/1990

Hendrik Petrus Bremmer
Leiden 1871-1956 The Hague
Still Life with Book and Ginger Jar
Canvas, 55 × 65.5 cm - 1894
Inv. S 418 M/1990

_____

Johan Joseph Aarts
The Hague 1871-1935 Amsterdam
Clearing in the Forest
Canvas, 29.4 × 44.5 cm - ca. 1895
Inv. S 429 M/1992

Aarts and Bremmer were among the first painters to espouse Seurat's Neo-impressionism in the Netherlands. They were preceded by Jan Toorop, who through his contacts with the Belgian circle of artists known as Les XX had been introduced to the principles of Pointillism at an early stage, and remained loyal to them until the early 1890s. As chairman of the painting section of the Haagsche Kunstkring, in 1892 he organised an influential exhibition of Neo-impressionists in The Hague, where work by Pissarro, Seurat, Signac and Van de Velde, among others, was displayed.

Aarts was primarily a graphic artist, but in 1895 he painted a series of landscapes in a Neo-impressionistic style, apparently under the influence of Henri Edmond Cross. Bremmer concentrated above all on still lifes, in which he employed a highly refined stipple technique to achieve subtle gradations of colour. Besides being a painter, Bremmer was also an influential critic who became one of the most important advocates of the work of Vincent van Gogh during the first decades of the twentieth century. As Mrs Kröller-Müller's advisor, moreover, he was instrumental in assembling one of the most superb collections of nineteenth-century art in the Netherlands, in which a large group of paintings and drawings by Van Gogh and five works by Seurat form the highpoints.

Leo Gestel
Woerden 1881-1941 Blaricum
Autumn Day
Canvas, 50 × 65 cm - 1909
Inv. S 38 B/1991, on loan from the
Rijksdienst Beeldende Kunst.

In the years leading up to World War I Leo Gestel was on the cutting edge of Dutch painting, along with Jan Sluijters and Piet Mondriaan. Around 1909/10 they explored ways of representing light by means of pure colour, thus breaking with the tonal manner of the Hague School in which Mondriaan and Gestel had originally been trained. Gestel's autumn landscape is characteristic of this 'luminist' period, as the new style was called.

Jan Sluijters
Bois-le-Duc 1881-1957 Amsterdam
Portrait of the Art Collector Beffie
Canvas, 108 × 86 cm - ca. 1910
Inv. S 68 B/1991, on loan from the
Rijksdienst Beeldende Kunst

Sluijters was awarded the Prix de Rome by the Amsterdam Rijksacademie. In Paris, where he stopped on his way back to Holland from a journey to Italy and Spain, he became fascinated by the painting of the 'Fauves', who broke completely with the dogmas he had imbibed in the course of his training. At the Rijksacademie the students had been more or less forbidden so much as to utter the name of Vincent van Gogh. The radical colour experiments of such painters as Derain, Matisse and Van Dongen, which caused such a furore that year in Paris, were apparently inspired by none other than Gauguin and Van Gogh.

To judge from the subject matter of the canvas and the handling of line, Sluijters's depiction of two women dancing is, like some of the work Picasso produced in the early 1900s, heavily indebted to Toulouse-Lautrec. *Femmes qui s'embrassent* was considered risqué on account of its crude manner and immoral air, and condemned in academic circles because of its 'contrived new tonality' and 'presumptuous disregard for beauty in the female forms'.

Jan Sluijters eventually became one of the most innovative Dutch artists of the first half of this century. Around 1910 he painted landscapes according to a variant of Neo-impressionism known as 'Luminism', which was inspired in part by Van Gogh. The artist was subsequently influenced by French Cubism, but ultimately evolved his own form of Expressionism characterised by robust nudes and pithy portraits. The expressive outlines and vivid palette of Sluijters's portrait of the collector Beffie attest to his profound admiration for Van Gogh.

Jan Sluijters
Femmes qui
s'embrassent
Canvas, 92 × 62.5 cm
1906
Inv. S 382 M/1987

Isaac Lazarus Israëls
Amsterdam 1865-1934 The Hague
Homage to Van Gogh
Canvas, 70.5 × 50.5 cm - 1917/20
Inv. S 233 V/1971

Along with Breitner, Isaac Israëls, son of Jozef Israëls, can be considered the principal member of the Amsterdam Impressionists. Though his own style did not reflect this taste, he was one of the first in the Netherlands to purchase work by Redon, and in 1889 he was already admiring the work of Van Gogh at the galleries of both Theo van Gogh and Tanguy in Paris. Israëls was a friend of Jo van Gogh-Bonger, of whom he painted several portraits. His homage to Van Gogh was painted in 1917-1920. During that period he had several pictures by Vincent in his studio, which the late artist's sister-in-law had lent him.

Van Gogh chronology

1853   Vincent van Gogh is born in Zundert on 30 March, the eldest son of the preacher Theodorus van Gogh (1822-1885) and Anna Cornelia Carbentus (1819-1907).

1857   His brother Theo is born on 1 May.

1869   Van Gogh joins the international art dealers Goupil & Cie in The Hague.

1872   His correspondence with Theo begins.

1873   In June Vincent is transferred to the firm's London branch, where he works until 15 May 1875.

1875   He is transferred – against his will – to Paris.

1876   Vincent is dismissed by Boussod & Valadon, who succeeded Goupil & Cie. He becomes a teacher at a boarding school in Ramsgate in mid-April. In July he moves to Isleworth, where as an assistant preacher he delivers his first sermon in October.

1877   Through April 1877 he works in a bookshop in Dordrecht. In May he moves to Amsterdam and prepares to study theology.

1878   In May Vincent abandons his studies in Amsterdam. He later moves to the Belgian Borinage to do evangelical work.

1880   Van Gogh decides to become an artist.

1881   In April Vincent moves in with his parents in Etten, where he spends much of his time drawing figures. His love for his cousin Kee Vos is unrequited.
In late November he moves to The Hague to study under his cousin Anton Mauve.

1882   In The Hague he rents a studio on Schenkweg. His relationship with Sien Hoornik, unmarried and pregnant, contributes to his falling out with Mauve. His uncle, the art dealer C.M. van Gogh, commissions twelve drawings with views of The Hague from him.

1883   His relationship with Sien Hoornik having come to an end, on 11 September Vincent leaves for the province of Drenthe. He concentrates on landscape. In early December he opts to go to his parents, who have moved to Nuenen in the meantime.

1884   Following in the footsteps of J.F. Millet, Van Gogh decides to become a painter of peasant life, and in January begins work on a series of weavers.

1885   He paints a series of fifty peasant heads, which ultimately lead to *The Potato Eaters*, his first 'masterpiece'.
His father, the Rev. Theodorus van Gogh, dies on 26 March. On 24 November the artist leaves for Antwerp, where he is influenced by the work of Rubens.

1886   Works after the model at the Antwerp academy, but finds the training pedantic. About 1 March Van Gogh leaves unexpectedly for Paris, where he moves in with his brother Theo, now the manager of the Montmartre branch of Goupil's. For three months he works in the studio of Fernand Cormon.
Van Gogh paints views of Montmartre and experiments with colour in the form of flower still lifes. He becomes acquainted with the work of Monticelli and the Impressionists.

1887   Vincent buys Japanese prints from Siegfried Bing and art supplies from Père Tanguy. His intimates include Louis Anquetin, Emile Bernard, Lucien Pissarro and Paul

Signac. In March/April he organises an exhibition of Japanese prints at the Café du Tambourin.

In the summer he works on the banks of the Seine and in the new suburb of Asnières.

1888 The busy life of Paris exhausts Van Gogh and on 19 February, in search of sun and relaxation, he sets out for the south. Quite by chance he lands in Arles (Provence).

In April Vincent paints a series of blossoming orchards.

In May he rents the 'Yellow House' but does not move in till autumn.

He visits the Mediterranean fishing village of Saintes-Maries-de-la-Mer. That summer he paints scenes of life on the land, *Harvest in La Crau* being the highpoint.

In anticipation of the arrival of his friend and colleague Paul Gauguin, who plans to share the 'southern atelier' with him, in August Van Gogh paints the *Sunflowers* to decorate the Yellow House.

Not until 23 October does Gauguin arrive. The two artists work side by side on landscapes for a time, but their personalities and artistic outlook are so different that they inevitably fall out. Van Gogh threatens Gauguin with a knife and on 23 December cuts off a piece of his own ear. He is admitted to the hospital in Arles.

1889 Having recovered, on 7 January Van Gogh returns to the Yellow House.

In February the inhabitants of Arles turn against Van Gogh. He is subsequently re-admitted to the hospital.

On 17 April Theo marries Johanna ('Jo') Bonger, the sister of his friend Andries.

In May Van Gogh places himself under the care of Dr Peyron at the asylum St-Paul-de-Mausole in nearby St-Rémy. His olive orchards and cypresses date from this period. While painting *Entrance to a Quarry*, however, he suffers yet another attack.

That autumn Van Gogh paints his *Reaper*, which incorporates the wheat field he could see from his room. He regains his self-confidence painting copies after works by Delacroix, Millet and Rembrandt.

1890 In December and January Van Gogh must endure further attacks, each of which lasts for one week. Meanwhile his reputation grows steadily.

On 31 January Theo's son is born and named after his uncle Vincent Willem. The Belgian artist Anna Boch buys one of Vincent's pictures from Theo.

In late February Van Gogh undergoes another crisis, this one lasting until late April. He now returns to motifs from his Nuenen period, entitled 'souvenirs of the north'.

In mid-May Van Gogh leaves for the village of Auvers-sur-Oise near Paris. On his way through the capital he finally meets his sister-in-law Jo.

In Auvers, the physician and amateur painter Paul Gachet keeps an eye on Vincent. The artist takes a room at the inn of Ravoux and proceeds to paint the small houses of the village with their thatched roofs, the town hall and the church.

His principal landscapes, now painted on a new, double-square format, describe the outstretched wheat fields around Auvers.

On 27 July Van Gogh shoots himself in the chest and dies two days later in the company of Theo. Among the mourners at his funeral on 30 July are Bernard, Lucien Pissarro and Tanguy.

1891 Theo dies on 25 January. Jo van Gogh returns to the Netherlands with the brothers' art collection.

1892 The first Van Gogh exhibition in the Netherlands at the Haagsche Kunstkring.

1905 A large Van Gogh exhibition is mounted in the Stedelijk Museum, Amsterdam, where much of the collection of Dr Vincent Willem van Gogh is displayed from 1930.

1914 Jo van Gogh publishes Vincent's collected letters to Theo.

1962 Establishment of the Vincent van Gogh Foundation.

1973 Opening of the Van Gogh Museum in Amsterdam.

Index of artists

INDEX OF ARTISTS

Bibliography

General nineteenth century

Robert Rosenblum et al., *Art of the Nineteenth Century. Painting and Sculpture*, New York 1984

Gabriel Weisberg, *The Realist Tradition: French Painting and Drawing 1830-1900*, Cleveland 1980

Ronald de Leeuw et al., *The Hague School: Dutch masters of the 19th century*, London 1983

Carel Blotkamp et al., *The age of Van Gogh: Dutch painting 1880 - 1895*, Zwolle 1990

Sophie Monneret, *L'Impressionnisme et son époque*, Paris 1978

John Rewald, *Post-Impressionism from Van Gogh to Gauguin*, New York 1956

John House et al., *Post-Impressionism. Cross-Currents in European Painting*, London 1979

Patricia Eckert Boyer et al., *The Nabis and the Parisian Avant-Garde*, New Brunswick 1988

Geneviève Lacambre et al., *French Symbolist Painters. Moreau, Puvis de Chavannes, Redon and their followers*, London 1972

Van Gogh: general

J.-B. de la Faille, *The works of Vincent van Gogh. His paintings and drawings*, Amsterdam 1970

Jan Hulsker, *The complete Van Gogh: paintings, drawings, sketches*, New York 1980

Jan Hulsker, *Vincent and Theo van Gogh: a dual biography*, Ann Arbor 1985

Louis van Tilborgh et al., *Vincent van Gogh: paintings*, Milan 1990

Griselda Pollock, *Vincent van Gogh in zijn Hollandse jaren. Kijk op stad en land door Van Gogh en zijn tijdgenoten 1870-1890*, Amsterdam 1980

Evert van Uitert et al., *Van Gogh in Brabant. Paintings and drawings from Etten and Nuenen*, Zwolle 1987

Bogomila Welsh-Ovcharov, *Vincent van Gogh. His Paris period 1886-1888*, Utrecht 1976

Bogomila Welsh-Ovcharov et al., *Van Gogh à Paris*, Paris 1988

Bogomila Welsh-Ovcharov, *Vincent van Gogh and the birth of Cloisonism*, Toronto 1981

Ronald Pickvance, *Van Gogh in Arles*, New York 1984

Ronald Pickvance, *Van Gogh in St. Rémy and Auvers*, New York 1986

Tsukasa Kodera, *Vincent van Gogh, Christianity versus Nature*, Amsterdam & Philadelphia 1990

Louis van Tilborgh et al., *Van Gogh & Millet*, Zwolle 1988

Tsukasa Kodera et al., *Vincent van Gogh and Japan*, Kyoto & Tokyo 1992

Roland Dorn et al., *Vincent van Gogh and the modern movement 1890-1914*, Freren 1990

John Rewald, 'Theo van Gogh as art dealer' in: *Studies in Post-Impressionism*, 1986, pp. 7-115

Van Gogh: letters

Han van Crimpen et al., *De brieven van Vincent van Gogh*, The Hague 1990

Douglas Cooper, *Paul Gauguin: 45 Lettres à Vincent, Théo et Jo van Gogh. Collection Rijksmuseum Vincent van Gogh, Amsterdam*, The Hague & Lausanne 1983

Cahiers Vincent

Published in collaboration with the Vincent van Gogh Foundation

1. Fieke Pabst, *Vincent van Gogh's poetry albums*, Zwolle 1988

2. Walter Feilchenfeldt, *Vincent van Gogh & Paul Cassirer, Berlin. The reception of Van Gogh in Germany from 1901 to 1914*, Zwolle 1988

3. Cornelia Peres et al., *A Closer Look: Technical and Art-Historical Studies on Works by van Gogh and Gauguin*, Zwolle 1991

4. Ronald Pickvance, *'A great artist is dead'. Letters of Condolence on Vincent van Gogh's Death*, Zwolle 1992

5. Louis van Tilborgh et al., *The Potato Eaters by Vincent van Gogh*, Zwolle 1993

The collection of the Van Gogh Museum

Evert van Uitert et al. (eds.), *The Rijksmuseum Vincent van Gogh*, Amsterdam 1987

Johannes van der Wolk, *The seven sketchbooks of Vincent van Gogh: a facsimile edition*, New York 1986

Josefine Leistra, *George Henry Boughton: God Speed! Pelgrims op weg naar Canterbury*, Zwolle 1987

Bogomila Welsh-Ovcharov, *Emile Bernard (1868-1941): the theme of bordellos and prostitutes in turn-of-the century French art*, New Brunswick 1988

Charlotte van Rappard-Boon et al., *Catalogue of the Van Gogh Museum's collection of Japanese prints*, Zwolle 1991

Ronald de Leeuw et al., *Van Gogh Museum. Aanwinsten/Acquisitions 1986-1991*, Zwolle 1991

Catalogues of exhibitions held in the Van Gogh Museum: a selection

Ronald Pickvance et al., *Monet in Holland*, Zwolle 1986

Ellen Wardwell Lee et al., *Neo-impressionisten: Seurat tot Struycken*, Zwolle 1988

Gianna Piantoni et al., *Ottocento/Novecento: Italiaanse kunst 1870-1910*, Zwolle 1988

Caroline Boyle-Turner et al., *Jan Verkade: hollandse volgeling van Gauguin*, Zwolle 1989

MaryAnne Stevens et al., *Emile Bernard 1868-1941: a pioneer of modern art*, Zwolle 1990

Patricia Eckert Boyer et al., *L'Estampe originale: artistic printmaking in France, 1893-1895*, Zwolle 1991

Ronald Pickvance, *Degas sculptor*, Zwolle 1991

Series 19th-century Masters

1. Ronald de Leeuw, *Philippe Rousseau 1816-1887*, Amsterdam & Zwolle 1993

2. Lucas Bonekamp, *Louis Welden Hawkins 1849-1910*, Amsterdam & Zwolle 1993

3. Charlotte van Rappard-Boon, *Félix Bracquemond 1833-1914*, Amsterdam & Zwolle 1993

4. Ian Millman, *Georges de Feure 1869-1943*, Amsterdam & Zwolle 1993

Colophon

Publisher:
Waanders Uitgevers, Zwolle

Design:
Gijs Sierman, Amsterdam

Translation:
Andrew McCormick

Printer:
Waanders Drukkers, Zwolle

© 1994 Uitgeverij Waanders b.v., Zwolle

CIP-gegevens Koninklijke Bibliotheek Den Haag

Leeuw, Ronald de

The Van Gogh Museum : Painting and Pastels / Ronald de Leeuw.
– Zwolle: Waanders – Ill.
Vert. van: Van Gogh Museum : schilderijen & pastels. -
Zwolle : Waanders 1993
ISBN 90-6630-405-7 geb.
NUGI 921/911
Trefw.: Van Gogh Museum (Amsterdam).

Many thanks to Vincent van Gogh-Stichting

Photos:
Vincent van Gogh-Stichting, Amsterdam except the following:
Amsterdams Historisch Museum (pp. 17-19);
Rijksdienst Beeldende Kunst, The Hague (pp. 13, 24, 28, 36, 38,
42, 44, 86, 97, 261, 262);
Rijksmuseum Amsterdam (pp. 18, 20, 21, 24, 25, 28, 30, 40, 81);
Rijksmuseum Kröller-Müller, Otterlo (p. 29);
Stedelijk Museum, Amsterdam (p. 8);
Van Gogh Museum, Amsterdam (pp. 6, 7, 10, 12, 19-21, 22-23, 26,
27, 31-35, 37, 39, 42-45, 47, 48 51-53, 61, 82, 85, 87, 93, 96, 103,
110, 112, 113, 118-1230, 134, 224, 242, 243, 245-248, 251, 253-
260, 263).